REGENSBURG AND AUGSBURG

The publication of this volume has been made possible through the generosity of the late

ABRAHAM ERLANGER

who died October 1, 1929, and who left a bequest to the Jewish Publication Society of America to be used "to defray the cost of writing or editing and publication of a specific work or works."

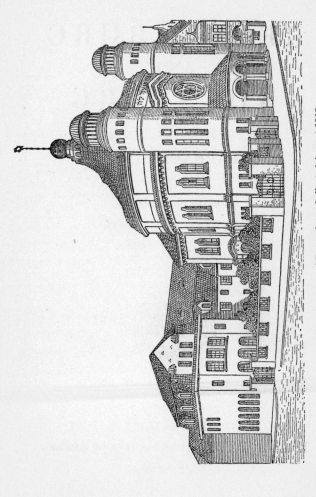

The modern synagogue of Regensburg dedicated August 1912.

JEWISH COMMUNITIES SERIES

REGENSBURG
AND
AUGSBURG

by RAPHAEL STRAUS

Translated from the German
by FELIX N. GERSON

PHILADELPHIA

THE JEWISH PUBLICATION SOCIETY OF AMERICA

1939—5699

**PRINTED IN THE UNITED STATES OF AMERICA
PRESS OF THE JEWISH PUBLICATION SOCIETY
PHILADELPHIA, PENNA.**

CONTENTS

LIST OF ILLUSTRATIONS

(Illustrations from *Zur Geschichte der Juden in Regensburg* by Isaak Meyer, Verlag Louis Lamm, Berlin 1913, now Amsterdam).

FOREWORD

THE work presented in the following pages is based in large measure upon unpublished sources found by the author in various German and Austrian archives. Some of these items are being published in the course of the preparation of this work and are to be issued under the title, *Records and Official Documents For a History of the Jewish Community of Regensburg Toward the End of the Middle Ages*. These excerpts will be cited in the following pages as *Straus I*. The items that will not have appeared in print are designated as *Straus, Material*. The matter to be published under the caption *Straus I* has already been utilized by the author in his publication, *Die Judengemeinde Regensburg im ausgehenden Mittelalter* (Heidelberg, 1932). This work will be cited in the following pages as *Straus II*. The author feels that a special bibliography is not required in this presentation. The works bearing on the subject are cited where references to them occur.

Jerusalem, November, 1934.

NOTE

No citation is made of a recently published work by Wilhelm Grau, *Antisemitismus im späten Mittelalter*, Munich, 1934, which is based entirely upon *Straus I*. This work, despite the support given it by the philosophical faculty of the University of Munich, is entirely valueless to scholars. The story of the origin of this publication deserves to be given here as a matter of record. In the Autumn of 1932, the student Wilhelm Grau called upon the author of the following pages, introducing himself as a candidate for the Doctor's degree and as desirous of preparing an exposition of the development of anti-Semitism during the Middle Ages along the lines of its manifestation in Regensburg. He asked for this purpose access to the source material of the author, revealing himself, without having been questioned in the matter, as a political Democrat who desired, after he had passed his examinations, to devote himself to liberal journalism. The change in the German mental attitude in 1933 has influenced this young man, as it has many older persons, and directed his activities along political lines. Should public opinion in Germany be subject to another change at a future period, he will doubtless be prepared to return to his former viewpoint. *Variis agimur illusionibus.*

REGENSBURG AND AUGSBURG

CHAPTER I

STATEMENT OF THE PROBLEM

BAVARIA has, next to Prussia, the largest area of any of the constituent states of the German Reich. Its territory comprises, in its present day expansion, about 29,000 square miles, which represents about one sixth of Germany's entire area. Augsburg and Regensburg are, compared with Munich, the capital city, the largest communities in Southern Bavaria. Augsburg is the residential government center of the district of Swabia, and Regensburg of the Upper Palatinate. The population, today, of the former city is about 165,000, of which number about 900 are Jews. The population of the latter city is about 76,000, with about 400 Jews. Both cities still have a distinctive economic and cultural character, which existed in still greater measure in former days. For this reason it is important to present the history of these cities from a comparative point of view. To treat each place separately would prove of less value inasmuch as the history of both cities, in relation to the fate of their Jewish communities, includes, as we shall see, uneventful periods in which few if any Jews are to be met and these few enjoying no security of livelihood. The Jewish communities of both cities have never sufficiently recovered from the misfortunes they suffered in the later Middle Ages to regain the prominent status they had enjoyed in former days.

1

One important reason for this lay in their proximity to the capital city of Munich (with about 9000 Jews in its population of 680,000). The unparalleled development enjoyed by this city in the course of the 19th century retarded the growth of its two small neighboring cities. As the center of gravity of Jewish development in Augsburg and Regensburg was in the past, whereas that of Munich began in the 19th century, we have refrained from presenting the Jewish history of Munich in similar detail in the present work. In view, however, of the close political association of these three South-Bavarian cities, we felt that we should not forgo a few passing references to the situation of the Munich community, especially in our treatment of the later spiritual development in the 19th century, in which Munich became in a very large measure representative of the adjacent terrain. A comparative view of this sort will afford a comprehensive picture of the Jewish past as well as the present.

In another sense, too, a comparative survey may prove of value. The changes in the development of the Jewish communities mirror the variations in the development of the cities as a whole. For this reason it is necessary to make a comprehensive survey of the development of the cities of Augsburg and Regensburg by way of orientation.

Regensburg was in the olden time what Munich became at a later period, the capital of the Bavarian dukes and, for a time, also of the German kings. But its importance in the period covered by the 10th to the 14th centuries was due not only to this political prominence, but primarily to its extensive commercial interests. It was favored in its contacts with both the West and the East by the navigable waters of the Danube, and for a lengthy period formed an important point of transfer for shipments between England, Flanders, the Champagne country, and Eastern European ports. For the northern and south-lying districts it formed an important connecting link between Venice, which was in the later Middle Ages the most important center of trade for Oriental merchandise, and the German and Slavic North and East. Its position as a capital city was maintained by Regensburg until the 10th century, and its rank as a leading trade center, until well into the 15th century. Eventually it relinquished its political supremacy to Munich and its rank as a commercial center to Augsburg, Nuremberg, Prague and Vienna. In the course of the 15th century — the period of Jewish expulsions — it fell into so pitiful a decline that it was compelled to relinquish temporarily its independent character, i. e. its sovereignty, and subordinate itself to the authority of the dukes of Munich. Inasmuch as the Emperor, jealous of the latters' supremacy, opposed this subordination, it ultimately continued its existence as a "free" city, though in a state of pitiful decadence. It was not until 1810 that, by the decree of Napoleon I, it became incorporated with Bavaria. After its decline in the later Middle Ages, it never again approached the importance of Munich and Augsburg. At the very time of its completest decadence Regensburg persecuted its Jewish inhabitants with the greatest virulence, ultimately expelling them from its territory.

After Munich had become, in the 12th century, the ducal residential city, Regensburg, despite its legal status as a "free" city, became in many respects a dependency of the duke. The duke had held from olden times many rights of sovereignty in Regensburg, among which was the right to levy taxes upon the Jews and the exercise of jurisdiction over them.[1] But greater than his legal authority were the actual powers exercised by him. For the free city of Regensburg was environed by Bavarian territory and was consequently compelled by its commercial interests alone to give consideration to Bavarian requirements. For the ducal rulers were able, not alone by means of military threats but by interference with shipping activities or the imposition of political tax levies, to enforce compliance with their demands, and frequently resorted to these methods of compulsion. In the history of the Jews of Regensburg, these matters affecting the city as a whole are clearly revealed. Until the end of the Middle Ages, when these conditions were changed through the termination of the authoritative ducal dynasty,[2] the Jews were enabled to profit by reason of dissensions that arose between the duke, the city, and the emperor, and it was on this account that their expulsion from Regensburg was later than from other cities. When this expulsion actually occurred in 1519, a number of the victims merely crossed the Danube bridge into the Regensburg "Suburb" (Stadtamhof), which belonged to Bavaria.

From the circumstance of the subordination of the Jews to the dukes of Bavaria, one might almost regard the medieval Jewry of Regensburg as the parent of the Jewish community of Munich. For the Jewish community of Munich itself did not come into existence until a relatively later period (after 1200), and never attained to the importance of the Regensburg community.

The Jewry of Augsburg had, indeed, in the 19th century, entered into a close association with that of Munich, this formerly free city having also been consolidated with Bavaria in 1806. But this association had been a much weaker one in the past. The city of Augsburg lies at the western boundary of the high Bavarian-Swabian plateau that forms the approach to the Alps. Its economic interests were directed toward the West and South as those of Regensburg toward the East and South. Augsburg was commercially more closely allied with the West than it was with Regensburg or Munich, for the city of Ulm, which had formerly also numbered a large Jewish community, is only about 80 kilometers distant.

Only occasionally had a closer relationship existed in the olden days between Augsburg and Munich; once in the time of the Emperor Louis the Bavarian (1314–47) and later in the days of Duke Frederick (1375–93). But in both these instances compelling political motives had been the cause of the closer alliance. In the former case the occasion was the election of the Duke of Munich to the German kingship, bringing about a direct political relationship to

the city at large and particularly to its Jewish inhabitants. The closer association with Duke Frederick
was consequent upon his investment as imperial
prefect of Swabia. Despite this temporary association of the city and its Jewish inhabitants with
Bavaria, the older development would rather suggest
our consideration of Augsburg in connection with
the Swabian municipalities. But the great development of Bavaria since the 16th century brought with
it a more intimate involvement of Augsburg with
the Bavarian interests. The city grew in modern
times, as had Regensburg at an earlier period, if not
into a legal, yet into an economical and political
dependence upon Bavaria. The more recent development of the city, therefore, justifies the inclusion of
the city of Augsburg in our present consideration.

In view of the limitation of this work to the
consideration of Southern Bavaria, we are omitting
three other Bavarian Jewish communities, those of
Nuremberg, Würzburg and Fürth. The relation
existing between these cities and the before-mentioned South Bavarian Jewries cannot be enlarged
upon at this time and can be accorded only occasional reference. Central-Southern Bavaria, however,
includes many smaller Jewries, which have but little
significance today, but which at times during the
past enjoyed considerable prominence. Such are
the Jewries of "Ries"; those of the Margravate of
Burgau, in part closely allied with the Augsburg
Jewish community; those of Passau, Straubing,
Deggendorf, Landshut, Ingolstadt, Freising, and
others. But these had only temporary significance

and can be accorded only passing reference in the following pages. There are isolated cases of Jewish residence in other small South Bavarian localities, such as Tölz, Dingolfing, Eggenfelden, Vilshofen, Mittenwald, Schärding, Landau, Plattling, Peratzhausen, Burghausen, Weilheim, Pfaffenhofen, Dietfurt, Kelheim, Reichenhall, Mosburg, Abach, Rietenburg, Abensberg, Wolnzach, Eching, etc., which cannot be considered here.

However, there are some of these rural and small-town Jewish settlements which cannot be left out of consideration. In the first centuries of the later period, during which no Jews were permitted to remain in Munich, Augsburg and Regensburg, or in most of the larger German cities, the Jews migrated in large numbers to neighboring localities under other domination; the descendants of the former Regensburg Jews being found in Stadtamhof and those of the former Augsburg Community in Steppach, Kriegshaber, Pfersee, Göggingen and Oberhausen. We may, therefore, speak of the continued residence, in these neighboring towns and villages, of the Jewish communities of Regensburg and Augsburg after their expulsion from these cities. In the case of Augsburg this would apply uninterruptedly from the time of the Jewish expulsion to the time of their official readmission. In the case of Regensburg, however, it would cover only a short period, as the Jews who sought refuge in Stadtamhof at the time of the expulsion in 1519 were compelled to vacate this place of refuge when, in 1551, the Jews were driven from the entire Bavarian territory.

The efforts made by the cities of Augsburg and Regensburg, following the later Jewish expulsions, to be entirely free of Jews, proved futile. This was owing to the fact that the anti-Jewish policy of the cities was continually thwarted by the interests of the authoritative rulers and high dignitaries, and at times the policy of the cities themselves was vacillating.[3] This vacillation was terminated when, at the Napoleonic conclusions of peace, both cities were placed under Bavarian domination, Augsburg in 1806 and Regensburg in 1810. With this change an entire reorganization of Bavarian State administration was inaugurated, including the regulation of the status of the Jews which was determined anew in the enactments of 1805 and of June 10, 1813.

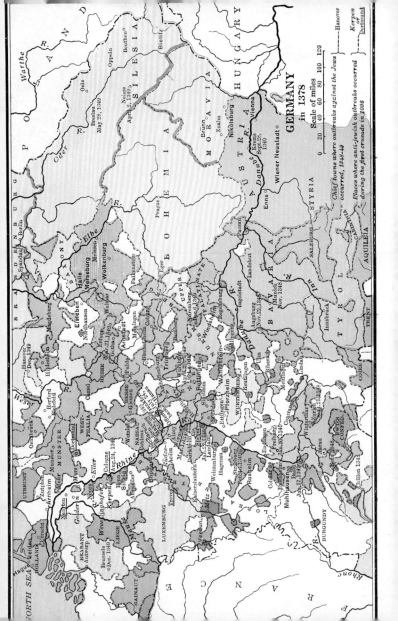

GERMANY
in 1378

Scale of miles
0 20 40 60 80 100 120

——— Chief towns where anti-jewish outbreaks against the Jews
occurred, 1348–49

– – – – Places where anti-jewish outbreaks occurred
during the first crusade in 1096

Hanover ———
Kerpen - - - -
Dortmund – – –

CHAPTER II

COMPARATIVE VIEW OF THE HISTORICAL DEVELOPMENT

A. POLITICAL DEVELOPMENT TO THE END OF THE MIDDLE AGES

THE origins of most of the German cities are shrouded in darkness. We do not know when the city of Regensburg was founded. Tradition traces its origin to prehistoric times, as far back as the ancestral Isaac.[4]

If, as is asserted, Jews were settled there in the remote days when *Castra Regina* (in German, Regensburg*) was a Roman military outpost, then it is clear that they were present in Regensburg centuries before the Bavarians themselves resided there. But there exist no authoritative records to this effect. The assertion made in the 15th century by both the Regensburg and Augsburg Jews that their forbears had resided in this locality for 1500 or perhaps 1800 years,[5] must undoubtedly be relegated to the realm of legend. The same is true of the assertion made by the Jews that the city's patron saint, St. Emeram, who lived about 700 C.E., was a Jew named Rabbi Amram[6] and was buried in the Jewish cemetery of Regensburg. It is not even certain that Jews had come to Regensburg with the Roman legionaries and had subsequently established a commercial settlement there. The earliest

---

*Regensburg also bore the name Ratisbon.

authentic records of Jewish settlement in German
marts of trade go back to the declining days of the
Roman Empire. In the following four centuries,
however, during the period of the national migrations and of the political readjustments of the time,
when the Bavarians, too, occupied the land which
later bore their name, we find no record of Jewish
commercial settlements in Germany. It was the
period of a reconstructed Central Europe, following
upon the storms that grew out of the general migration of peoples. The legal enactments of Charle-
magne (died 814) suddenly illuminate, after an
extended period of darkness, the conditions affecting Jewish life and affairs. The present day East
Bavarian and upper Austrian countries were consolidated by this monarch with the western portions
of his empire. It is in this period that we find the
first records in Salzburg, which later became the
archbishopric having authority over Regensburg,
and it is in this time that we should like to place the
foundations of a healthy and growing settlement of
Jews in Regensburg. It is likely that there were
earlier beginnings, but not farther back than the
Merovingian period, for any settlements of Roman
days could not have withstood the disintegration
caused by the widespread migrations of the nations.
The first actual record of Jews in Regensburg dates
from the year 981, of Jews in Augsburg from 1212.[7]

The location of the Jewish quarter in Regensburg
sheds a clearer light upon the history of this community. Until the time of the Jewish expulsion of
1519, this quarter was located within the wall sur-

rounding the former Roman barracks and could therefore not have been in existence before the evacuation of this military post. It is situated directly on the line of the main thoroughfare where this extends toward the barracks, an especially favorable location for traffic. The bridge that connected the gate of the barracks and the subsequently erected city gate, and which spanned a narrow rivulet, was named the Jews' Path up to the time of the later Middle Ages. Somewhat more advantageously located was the Italian quarter, occupied by traders who had migrated from the South. This was not directly on the line of the main thoroughfare, but in near proximity, and was sheltered by the western wall of the barracks. This situation would indicate that the Italians were the first to occupy the city, and that the Jews came shortly afterward; also that the later German-Christian citizens settled there as artisans and husbandmen under the protection of the comital, later the ducal court, without any connection with the independent commercial community.

With the growth of a Christian citizenry, the Christian city impinged upon the Jewish section of the town and commercial contacts in the market place grew into intimate neighborly relations. In immediate proximity to the Jewish section stood the Augustinian convent, and the Jewish quarter was barely 250 meters distant from the cathedral. Christian sections bounded the Jewish city on the north, the west and the south. When the relations between these people assumed an unfriendly phase, this proximity became a thorn in the flesh. The condition of the Jews had grown less favorable in the course of time. Development of traffic on the Danube, the presence of the cathedral and the market had diverted the commercial center of gravity toward the north. Nevertheless, the continued prosperity of the Jews led to hostility in periods of Christian-Jewish tension.

Indubitable indication of the great age of the Jewish section of Regensburg is found in the extended network of its sub-cellars. It is supposed that underground passage-ways connected all the Jewish houses of the town, and at the time of the destruction of these buildings in 1519 and the reconstructive work in the 18th century, the discoverers of the underground passages were amazed at finding these old time labyrinths, which they looked upon as offering evidence of secret criminal activities.[8] This assumption has been given credence even in the most recent historical writing. If it is recognized that these underground passage-ways were constructed as places of refuge in troublous times (the earlier and the later Middle Ages are not considered as the building period), our assumption that the Jewish quarter was founded in the disturbed period of a pagan age receives distinct confirmation.

The location of the Jewish quarters in Augsburg and in Regensburg indicates perhaps that the latter settlement was the elder of the two. The Regensburg quarter occupying, as we have shown, a very desirable part of the city, must have enjoyed a more

or less substantial organization in the period preceding the establishing of the Christian community.
The Jewish quarter of Augsburg, however, though
also located on the main thoroughfare, was, in its
proximity to the cathedral area and to the city's
fruit market, on episcopal territory. This was the
location known to have existed as early as 1259.
In Regensburg the relative locations of the several
sections were the cathedral, the Christian community, the Jewish quarter; in Augsburg, however,
the cathedral, the Jewish quarter, and the Christian
community. Had Augsburg been a relatively young
city and princely foundation, as Landshut had
been, for example, the location of its Ghetto would
have led to the conclusion that the Jews had been
part of the original settlers of the city. But this
cannot be considered in the case of Augsburg, and
it must be taken for granted that its Jews had been
permitted to settle there under ecclesiastical protection at a period in which a Christian community
was already in existence. But the correctness of
this assumption could be maintained only upon the
basis that there had been no change of residence of
the Jews in this city. A situation of this nature is,
for instance, revealed in Landshut in the 15th
century.[9] It may easily have been the case that
the Jewish quarter of Augsburg had been formerly
located in another part of the city and that after
the destruction of 1241 there was a removal to a
point nearer to the cathedral site.

The first reference to Jews in Augsburg is found
in the year 1212, and is therefore definitely of more

recent date than the earliest Regensburg records.
Can this be merely a lacuna in the records, or did
the Jewish settlements in Augsburg really take
place at a much later period? At about the end of
the 9th century, a reference is found that would
indicate the likelihood of the presence of Jews in
Augsburg at that time.[10] We possess no definite
knowledge of their first appearance in this city.

The early phases of the city of Munich lie in a
much later period. Duke Henry conveyed to the
inhabitants of this village, for political reasons,
certain rights, especially that of the traffic in salt
with the neighboring salt mining district. By this
action he created a class of Christian citizens and
was enabled to dispense with the Jews, who were
generally attracted by the opportunities afforded by
such new establishments. A different attitude had
been taken by Duke Louis in the organization of
the South Bavarian capital of Landshut in 1204.
He had invited the participation of Jews in order
to secure a commercial development for the newly
founded city.

The Jews played an insignificant part in the development of Munich as a municipality, as their homes
at that period lay at a considerable distance—
barely 300 meters from the ducal palace, to be sure,
but quite considerable when it is remembered that
the city at that time covered but a limited area.

If we wonder whence the Jews came who settled
in Regensburg and Augsburg at a very early
time and came to Munich and Landshut at a
relatively later period, we must rely upon con-

jectures. Jewish names found at a later period in
Regensburg bear evidence of Czechic origin. Commercial relations of Jews with Bohemia existed at
an even earlier period. There is no basis for an
assumption that only Bohemian Jews had composed the earlier settlement in Regensburg, but it
cannot be doubted that they comprised a considerable number of these settlers. The path taken by
the Jews was similar in this case to the channels of
trade that wound eastward from Regensburg
through Bohemia, and was the same as that by
which the Bavarians themselves had come to this
region.

If one assumes in the case of Augsburg a similar
conformity in the paths of Jewish migration with
the roads of commerce, one must conclude that the
older Jewish settlement of Augsburg was recruited
from western and southwestern points. At a later
period the records reveal various interrelations
between the Jews of Ulm and Augsburg, which
would confirm the western origin of this migration.

The origin of the Jews who settled in Munich
and Landshut cannot be as definitely determined
owing to the unquestionably small number of the
settlers. It has been assumed that a number of the
Jews who had been expelled from France in the
year 1180 had come to Munich.[11] This is probably
the case. But one does not need to go so far afield.
In Germany itself the Jews had grown uneasy during the second and third crusades (1146 and 1188).
It is probable that at least some of these Jews came
from Regensburg, as this city was not far distant

and had political relations with the reigning dukes. It is also significant that the name of the first Regensburg Jew given in the records is Abraham of Munich.[12]

We note, therefore, that it was not before the year 1200 that the mists which had obscured the origins of the Regensburg-Augsburg Jewish settlements begin to dissolve. There are suddenly revealed in the light of history descriptions of a more or less completed organization, with religious worship, synagogue, burial ground and ritual bath. At the same period there is brought to clearer recognition a knowledge of the Christian civic organizations; the most important motif of the subsequent historic development being constituted by the periodic friendly and antagonistic relations between the Jewish and Christian communities.

This historic development, too, assumed different phases in Munich from the form it took in Augsburg and Regensburg. In Munich, as the ducal seat, the influence of the rulers was and continued to be a decisive factor. In the same measure as they had invited an immigration of the Jews, they determined the legal status of their residence and expelled them when it was deemed expedient. On the other hand, the cities of Augsburg and Regensburg had in the 13th century become free cities, i. e. they had secured sovereignty in matters relating to their communal regulations. In both cities the former jurisdiction of the reigning bishops in the affairs of the Jewish inhabitants had been eliminated since that time. In both cities, too, the competition of the citizens became the leitmotif of Jewish existence. While this motif was also present in the affairs of Munich, it was much less in evidence. For only a brief period did the rapid supremacy of the Munich Christian community over the Jews prove effective. When, about 1400, it rebelled against the ducal power, it suppressed, as had the other cities, the commercial privileges of the Jews. The dukes, however, maintained their supremacy. And though they did not actually favor the Jews — they had, it is true, accorded them in 1416 the privilege of establishing a burial ground, which was located in the vicinity of the present day Massman Place — their supremacy restrained to some extent the anti-Semitic activities of the Christian citizenry.

In the cities of Regensburg and Augsburg the tension existing between the Christian and Jewish communities ran along parallel lines. As long as the local patriciate retained an established control, the Jews were protected against attacks of the mob. The Jews were protected, too, against encroachments on the part of the clergy, such as summons to appear before ecclesiastical courts in connection with church laws against usury. Cities and Jews alike preferred the secular courts. In both cities the security of the Jewish status was weakened to the degree in which the older wealthy patriciate suffered a decline in its authority.

In Augsburg an understanding was reached, in 1380, between the patriciate and the rebellious guilds, by which the latter were given participation in the government. The continued presence of the

patricians in the municipal government, though
with diminished influence, prevented a reversion to
reactionary Jewish policies.

In Regensburg, in the year 1349, at the time of
the widespread Jewish persecutions, 247 of the leading citizens of the community organized to give
assurance of protection to the Jews;[13] an assurance
that appears to have proven effective. This state of
affairs remained in force over a lengthy period, so
that this city was among the last to participate in
the Jewish expulsions.

Of both Augsburg and Regensburg it is related
that pestilence, food scarcity and commercial and
political disasters preceded the Jewish expulsions.[14]

These conditions are in no instance specifically
referred to as the causes of the expulsions, but must
be regarded as having been the occasion of bringing
them about, as this misfortune overtook the Jews
at specific periods. The contrary is true of the
religious movements that marked this period, which
resembled in this respect the period of the crusades.[15]
Religious tensions formed the background and lent
impetus and sanction to the Jew-hatred that swept
over the municipalities.

These circumstances, which were merely contributing factors in the municipal Jewish expulsions
from Augsburg and Regensburg, were the decisive
causes in the ducal expulsions of the Jews from
Munich (1442). As far back as the classic period of
Jewish expulsions, the ruling princes could follow
their personal inclinations in the matter of protect-
ing or driving out the Jews of their domains. The

individual motives are entirely hidden. As there
was no reason why the dukes of Munich should feel
bound to comply with the demands of the citizens,
the clerical anti-Semitism of that time must be regarded as the predominating motive. This conclusion is also indicated by the fact that the duke's
physician who received the synagogue building as a
gift had a chapel dedicated to St. Damian erected
upon its site. Light may be thrown on this matter
by a brief consideration of Jewish policy pursued by
the Landshut ducal line as revealed by its four representatives in the 15th century: the Dukes Frederick,
Henry, Louis and George. Frederick, as a relative
and intimate of King Wenceslaus, was authorita-
tively identified with the latter's brusque fiscal
Jewish policy. He shared responsibility for the
financial and the resulting political disintegration
of the Jews. His son, Henry, who was by inherit-
ance the protector of Regensburg Jewry from 1447
until the time of his death, was reproached by his
contemporaries for having been "too devoted to
deer-stalking and the Jews". He protected the
Jews with all his might. One of the first official
acts of his son Louis, however, was to drive the Jews
out of his lower Bavarian territory. In the latter
part of his reign he made many efforts at proselytizing the Jews of Regensburg, and is believed at
times to have contemplated their expulsion. Of his
son George it is reported, on the other hand, that
he made efforts to protect the Regensburg Jewry.
Among the larger Jewish communities of that time,
only those of Straubing and Munich were in the

direct control of Duke Albrecht of Munich, and he destroyed both of them. Though we recognize these largely divergent motives that brought about the expulsions of Jews from the Dukedom of Munich on the one hand and the municipal expulsions from Augsburg and Regensburg on the other, a common influence should not be overlooked, namely the prevailing spirit of the age. Jewish expulsion was a watchword that swept from Magdeburg to Vienna, throughout the German empire. The citizens of Regensburg subsequently complained that their efforts at Jewish expulsion had been curbed, whereas many of the other cities had been permitted to expel their Jewish inhabitants long before.[16]

Differences also manifested themselves in the conditions that followed the Jewish expulsions from the above-named three cities. The victims, especially the wealthier ones, simply crossed the Danube bridge from Regensburg into the neighboring Bavarian Stadtamhof, where, it is asserted, they came within a short time to be landowners of half the city. They became "metics" instead of "inhabitants", as a contemporary chronicler puts it. This condition, which restricted in large measure the scope of the Jewish expulsions, did not, however, continue over an extended period, as already in 1551 the Jews throughout the whole of Bavaria, including also those of the "Suburb" of Regensburg, as this city had been designated of old, were driven from their homes. Those expelled from Augsburg also found asylum in near proximity to the city. As they were enabled to remain in their new quarters until the time of the Jewish emancipation, it can be maintained that the Jewry of Augsburg never lost its continuous identity as an economic factor.

The small Jewish community of Munich, however, was entirely extinguished from the time of the expulsion (1442), as there were no alien demesnes lying in proximity to the gates of the ducal city in which the Jews could have found refuge.

B. POLITICAL CONDITIONS OF THE JEWS IN STATE AND CITY

At the period in which the Jews of these three cities appear in the pages of history, they occupied in general an identical political position, but characteristic differences marked detailed phases of their existence.

An understanding of their organization is made clearer by the fact of their segregation in a *vicus Judaeorum* which, separated by its own gates from the Christian community, had the characteristics of a city. In Regensburg and Augsburg the area of the Jewish quarters embraced a number of lanes. In their segregation the Jews administered their own affairs not only, as a matter of course, in the sphere of religious practice, but also in matters of taxation, and in purely Jewish law cases. There were even vestiges found[17] of an autonomous Jewish capital jurisdiction, evidently a survival from an older period, having no practical significance in the earlier and later Middle Ages. Civil jurisdiction in Christian-Jewish legal disputes in Regensburg was developed from a foundation of long existing tradition. The court consisted of a Christian judge nominated by the Jews and appointed by the duke, assisted by Christian and Jewish assessors of equal number.[18] Strictly Jewish affairs came under the jurisdiction of the rabbis and *parnasim* of the congregations, the latter being designated in most cases as revenue collectors, also as leaders or the "best" (Hebrew, *Tobim*), the former, in German, as *Meister* or *Hochmeister*. The function of the *parnasim* was to assess the tax upon the individuals bound to pay and to turn over the receipts to the treasury, i. e. the "Fiscus". The executive agent was the beadle (*Schulklopfer*). This functionary also acted as executor in legal transactions, especially in pronouncing the ban of excommunication (*Herem*) in the synagogue. In the period of our survey, these regulations had no permanent practical validity, but were subject to continual interference through arbitrary enactments. In the 15th century, especially, the disintegration of the regulations in Regensburg is clearly indicated in the sources.[19]

The admission of Jews from other sections held an important interest for the community in the matter of revenue. Inasmuch as the tax assessment was determined in a lump sum for the entire Jewish community, this immigration of "substantial", i. e. wealthy Jews, was of interest not only to the members of the Jewish community, who hoped by this means to lighten their individual burdens,

but also to the government, which beheld in this
accession a greater guarantee for tax payments and
a likelihood of increasing this source of revenue.
Of special importance in this connection was the
function of those officially associated with the
admission of these immigrants. This duty was on
this account generally withdrawn from the functions
of the *parnasim* and transferred to confidential
agents of the government. In the 15th century,
inroads by the government affecting the autonomy
of the Jewish community in every aspect were of
frequent occurrence. Fundamentally, however, the
rule was maintained that the Christian officials
could deal legally with Jewry as a whole only and
not with individual persons or causes.

The duties of the Jews were not restricted to the
paying of taxes. Until the year 1400 they were also
required to perform guard duty and construction
of fortifications *in persona* — a requirement from
which they were subsequently relieved through
money payments — on the ground that every one
who enjoyed the protection of the community should
make a contribution to the public welfare. For this,
however, it was necessary from time to time to
secure from the Emperor, as the supreme protector
of the Jews, special authorizations. Only since the
beginning of the 13th century are such authorizations (privileges) recorded in the annals of Regensburg and Augsburg, and they provide evidence of
the greater age of the ducal and episcopal legal
rights over the Jews, the origin and scope of which
are shrouded in darkness.

The manifold political rights over the Jews were determined by prevailing political conditions. The simplest development was presented in Munich, where the clerical and civic power did not come into conflict with the ducal authority. It is probably owing to this situation that we know so much less of the vicissitudes of the comparatively small Jewish community of Munich in the Middle Ages than we do of those in the imperial cities of Augsburg and Regensburg, in which the controversies between the conflicting powers shed considerable light upon the situation.

Characteristic are the differences between Augsburg and Regensburg in respect to the changes in the sovereignty exercised over the Jews.

In Regensburg, until the end of the Middle Ages, various rulers participated in the Jewish sovereignty, resulting in conflicts of authority, with harmful consequences for the Jews, such as the levying of higher taxes; but proving of advantage at the same time, inasmuch as these conflicts enabled the Jews, in certain emergencies, to array one ruling power against the other.

In this city the Bavarian dukes had originally shared with the bishops many rights of sovereignty, and among these was included control over the Jewish community. During the 13th century the bishop withdrew from this participation. In his stead the city council acquired a variously extended but never precisely determined participation in the direction of Jewish affairs. It exacted money from the Jews for general protection and acquired from the dukes and the bishops, until the 15th century, their civic and their Jewish jurisdiction. In the 15th century the Jewish magistrates, proposed originally by Jewish leaders and appointed to office by the dukes, were given identical standing with the municipal magistracy, i. e. the bailiffs and provosts, formerly ducal and episcopal judges respectively. These sat in judgment in the synagogue together with Jewish and Christian assessors. They represented also a court of appeal in disputes of distinctively Jewish import. Against the will, although without energetic opposition, of the ducal authority, this judicial arrangement was discontinued in the second half of the 15th century, so that by the end of the century the Jewish court in its distinctive form became non-existent. Until the time of the Jewish expulsion of 1519, no agreement was reached among the several interested parties (Jews, city, dukes, Emperor) concerning the reorganization of the Jewish court. At the same time there were withdrawn the other privileges granted the Jews by the ducal authority, namely safe conduct and admission of incoming Jews. The interest of the dukes in Jewish taxes was of course continued, but even these levies became practically ineffectual, as the Jews had become impoverished and were unable to meet these requirements.

Quite different was the development in Augsburg, where the municipal council had already in 1270 secured from King Conradin undivided control of Jewish affairs, exclusive of the episcopal and immediate royal authority, the supremacy of the latter being uninterrupted. To a restricted extent only there continued in existence, by reason of contradictory acts of royal favoritism, an episcopal control. There is no certainty that this authority was exercised upon the Jewish inhabitants of Augsburg, it being more probably restricted to the Jews of other parishes, notably Dillingen. The circumstance that authority over the Jews of Augsburg was definitely fixed even before the Interregnum, with which the general political disintegration of Germany in the Middle Ages began, had important consequences. The municipal law of Augsburg of 1276 regulated also Jewish affairs,[20] especially the economical, with a thoroughness that developed into a precedent. The cities of Munich and Nördlingen were subsequently, through King Louis, regulated upon the plan of the Augsburg Jewry law. It was thought that the frequent reference made to the Augsburg Jewry law indicated that the Jewish community of this city had enjoyed a peculiarly high standing, even as compared with Regensburg. This is, however, a misconception. In other localities, especially in Regensburg, the economic importance of the Jews could hardly have been less significant. But the political circumstances were much less favorable for the enactment of a comprehensive municipal Jewry law. In the meantime the imminently impending political disintegration prevented the continued development of Jewry law in Augsburg as well. There, also, the development of Jewry law no longer kept abreast of the economic development of the 14th century.

C. The Actual Legal Protection
of the Jews

The practical effectiveness of legal enactments is
dependent upon the good will and efficiency of
those entrusted with their enforcement. To maintain the legal protection accorded the Jews it required the coöperation of efficient municipal authorities. This coöperation could be either strengthened
or prejudiced; from above by the attitude of the
ruling powers, namely the clergy, the Emperor or
the local rulers, and from below by pressure brought
to bear upon the independent action of the rulers
by the body of the population. In default of either
of these circumstances the condition of the Jews was
endangered. In the case of the two cities with
which we are here concerned, it would be entirely
misleading to give credence to the oft-repeated
statement that the Jews of the Middle Ages possessed no legal rights. It is true, however, of these
two cities also that in consequence of manifold
disturbances the Jews were often practically outlawed. In general, the legal protection of the Jews
was more effectively maintained in strong govern-
ments than in weaker ones, and proved easier in
peaceful times than in times of disorder. This is
readily discernible in the history of the Jews of
our two cities.

In Regensburg, in 1097, in the troubled times of
the crusades, Jews who had been compelled to
accept baptism were permitted by the Emperor
Henry IV to return to the Jewish fold.[21]

There are no available records of the fate of the Jews of Augsburg and Regensburg during the period of the later crusades. Considering the relative importance of these Jewish communities we may conclude from this silence that nothing of significance had occurred. It is not unlikely that there were some bloody uprisings, but none of those major conflicts that would have been of historic moment.

In Augsburg the peaceful status was further safeguarded by the fact that this city at the time of the former Hohenstaufen Emperors possessed the character of a capital, and the legal protection of the Jews was associated with their fiscal interests, that is with the relationship of *servi camerae*, which had been definitely inaugurated by these Emperors.

In the period of later Jewish persecutions (1298, 1337, 1348–49), the governing authority in both cities was powerful enough to maintain the legal protection of the Jews. The imperial authority, which in Jewish affairs was supreme, had been, it is true, considerably weakened at that time. To maintain the legal protection of the Jews meant the maintaining of order in municipal affairs. It implied at the same time, however, the avoiding of difficulties with the higher ranking imperial protectors of the Jews. When, in the popular uprisings of 1348, the actual protection of the Jews became uncertain, Augsburg and Regensburg secured themselves through imperial and Bavarian guarantees against reprisals in case any harm should befall the Jews. At that time Augsburg Jewry was dis-

membered, but that of Regensburg was protected.
The cause of the difference in the history of these
two communities is not clear, but may be conjectured. In the first place, an economic crisis in the
first two decades of the century which had its
beginning in Italy had also affected Augsburg.
Secondly, the city as partisan of King Louis was
involved in the great money outlays which he had
to make by reason of his constant warfare and the
ecclesiastical ban under which he lay. These two
facts combined to put the city in the debt of the
Jews. Already in 1337 the Jews had been compelled
by the Emperor to give up to the city various documents, of which no clear description is given, but
which were no doubt bonds of indebtedness.[22] It
must be presumed that the indebtedness of the city
to the Jews weakened its will to protect them from
destruction in 1348. A monastic contemporary
says of the "Black Death" persecutions of the Jews
that: "It was their wealth that brought about the
destruction of the Jews. Had they been poor and
had they not been creditors of the sovereigns, they
would not have been brought to death at the
stake." A self-seeking, prodigal Augsburg Burgomaster, Heinrich Portner, who was personally
indebted to the Jews, is said to have been directly
responsible for the failure to protect them. This
is not improbable, as the situation was not such
that the Jews would have been delivered to destruction without opposition.

Special and individual circumstances also were
contributing factors in the return of the Jews to

Augsburg in 1350. The Emperor Karl declared
that the Jews of Augsburg had been unjustly con-
signed to the flames. Jews were also soon thereafter
found in Munich, but whence they came is not
recorded. This willingness to permit a return of the
Jews would indicate that they came from nearby
places.

Regensburg conducted in those days a consistent
Jewish immigration policy. It directed the rich
Jewish widow Chändlein and her business associates
to effect an agreement with the incoming Jews in
matters of tax payments.[23] This unconstitutional,
independent Jewish policy on the part of the city
reveals the actual weakness of the reigning dukes
of Munich.

Similarly, as the municipal authorities were
required to furnish protection to the Jews, the
latter were compelled to coöperate with the cities
in defensive measures adopted against their enemies.
Reference has been made above to the obligation
resting upon the Jews of Regensburg to participate
in guard duty and construction of fortifications.
That this obligation was actually enforced at an
earlier period is indicated by the fact that the Jews
of Augsburg had, in consideration of protection
accorded them in 1298, been required to construct
the so-called Jewish bastion, i. e. a section of the
city's fortifications, which remained in existence
until well into the 18th century. These were located
in the vicinity of the Church of the Holy Cross and
the Jewish burial ground. Whether the work on
these fortifications was actually participated in by

Jewish hands or whether Jewish money was exacted
for these operations is not revealed.

The cities exercised a greater participation in the
reorganization of the Jewish settlements after the
year 1350. The new settlements were established
in a period of improved economic conditions and
a consequent increase of municipal power, while
many nobles and citizens of lower rank were impoverished and became deeply involved in debt to the
Jews. During this period Regensburg extended
many privileges to the Jews to the disadvantage of
the ducal and episcopal prerogatives. There was a
prevailing tendency in Regensburg and elsewhere
in the latter half of the century to welcome Jews of
wealth, just as a few decades later it became the
practice to drive out the impoverished Jews.

A glance at this development reveals to what an
extent the condition of the Jews had been affected
by the happenings of 1348. Fundamentally, the
legal status of the Jews remained the same, but in
practice Regensburg had acquired in these days, at
the expense of the duke, a continually stronger
authority in the control of Jewish affairs, until a
century later the power of the city suffered a set-
back and the situation of the Jews changed again.

The increasing municipal influence which had
about 1360 definitely developed with the city's
commercial prosperity, while of immediate advantage, resulted disastrously in the long run. The
advantageous development was due to an increasing need of capital, which strengthened the standing
of Jewish banking houses. This brought with it an

attitude of carelessness in the matter of contractual indebtedness, which subsequently led to disputes and recriminations. The greater influence of the city's position led in the end to still another impairment of Jewish interests. What had been of advantage in the time of prosperity, turned in days of depression to misfortune for the Jews: subjection to an impoverished, embittered, incited populace (*Gemeinen*).

A clear picture of this development, in both its phases, is found in the Regensburg sources, more so than in those of Augsburg and Munich. This is due to the fact that the expulsion of the Jews from Regensburg came later than those of the two other cities, a circumstance which allowed the development to mature and be written up in the Humanistic period to which we owe so many historical sources. In Augsburg (1438) and Munich (1442) the development was cut off before that time.

The Jews participated in the growing economic importance of the cities. A definite policy that had for its purpose the attracting of wealthy Jews to their domains was adopted by Regensburg and Augsburg. Munich, of relatively lesser commercial importance, was by the operation of this policy thrust into the background. Among other Jews who had been induced to take up their residence in Regensburg was the wealthy Gnendl, and complaint was lodged by Duke Stephen against both cities that he had been subjected to "insult", i. e. a lack of consideration, by the enticing of the Jews from his domain. This new municipal Jewish policy was

definitely determined by practical considerations.
The cities included in the Swabian municipal con-
federacy were compelled to engage in serious conflicts with the nobility and knightly bodies to maintain the security and enlargement of their municipal
independence. For this purpose the money of the
Jews was required and to secure these funds it was
necessary to allow the Jews to earn it in their own
way, namely by giving them opportunities for
profitable business enterprises.

The cities were not particularly fond of these
enterprises or of the persons who conducted them.
They granted the Jews only a limited right of domicile, and reserved the right to expel them when they
should prove of no further use. The departure of
wealthy Jews, however, was prevented by their
arrest and imprisonment when they manifested a
desire to emigrate. This was a far-reaching limitation of Jewish liberty of movement, and was made
effective despite the fact that Regensburg had confirmed such freedom to them by municipal letters
of protection.

It appears, however, that their money was never
taken from the Jews by force. When in 1384 the
city of Nördlingen massacred its Jews and confiscated their belongings, this city was expelled from
the confederation, in which Regensburg and Augsburg were very influential. When King Wenceslaus
in 1385 and 1390 endeavored to secure a large portion of Jewish property by a cancellation of the
obligations of indebtedness to the Jews, the cities
registered an emphatic protest. In Augsburg the

King was able to achieve his purpose only by force, by ordering the arrest of Christian citizens. The cities feared not only the loss of Jewish taxes through the interference of the rulers, but also deprivation of their municipal independence through the establishment of royally protected Jewries within their territory, an eventuality they had reason to apprehend as a consequence of the efforts made by the King to establish a direct understanding between the Jews and the royal emissaries. This danger was more pronounced in the case of Regensburg, as the King had designated his emissaries as "Jew-protectors". The danger for the city was intensified by the fact that, by reason of family relationship, the King was assured of the assent of the dukes of Munich, who had control of the Jews of Regensburg. As was the case in many other cities, Regensburg and Augsburg were also finally compelled to yield to the claims made by the King upon these revenues. The cities had, besides, been subjected to military attacks and defeats by their enemies.

The advantages accruing to the Jews through the favorable policy of the cities were manifested between 1350 and 1390 in extended business opportunities and a temporary affluence. This had aroused the cupidity of the King. The advantages, therefore, did not prove of long duration. The disadvantages, however, that developed from this new supremacy of the cities in Jewish affairs proved more lasting. The cities, as was also the case in Regensburg and Augsburg, thwarted, by limitation of business activities, all attempts on the part of

the Jews to engage in mercantile pursuits, prohibiting at the same time their business of money-lending,
which was stigmatized as unethical. The latent
animosity toward the Jews was further aggravated
by the ecclesiastical reform synods—Duke William
of Munich was the imperially commissioned Protector of the Synod of Constance—in which Jewish
questions were frequently discussed. The Jews had
either to be very wealthy so as to purchase continued
toleration, or the prevailing economic condition of
the cities so favorable that they would have been
spared in any event. Both these conditions were
lacking. In Augsburg, following a previous economic crisis, the population of the city was decimated
by a great epidemic in 1436, intensifying the distress already precipitated by political disturbances.
The Jews were driven from the city in 1438, the
council having secured ratification from King
Albrecht for this procedure. The city of Regensburg was in a state of extreme political and economic
distress when in 1476 it contemplated the expulsion
of the Jews, which was finally put in effect in 1519.
There also, the persecutions of 1476 were preceded
by an epidemic.

CHAPTER III

ECONOMIC ACTIVITIES OF THE JEWS UNTIL THE END OF THE MIDDLE AGES

The first records of any substantial commercial activities of the Jews of Regensburg and Augsburg are found at a time when these activities were restricted to money-lending. Evidence of a developed trade in goods by the Jews of Regensburg at an early period is furnished by a Privilege accorded by Emperor Frederick in 1182, which granted the Jews permission to trade "in goods of every kind in the old manner", especially however, in gold, silver and other metals. The reference to trading in metals indicates that this traffic was especially in the hands of the Jews. No accounts of greater detail are found in any other sources of Jewish business activity. The so-called "Raffelstetten Tax Ordinance" of about 906, which regulated the Bavarian tax levies at the adjacent eastern boundary of Regensburg, specifically designates the Jews as export merchants. It is possible that the document had no particular reference to the Jews of Regensburg, but it would be inadmissible to exclude from the designation the Jews of this city, the largest and nearest-lying mart for the western and eastern traffic and the industrial center of the Jewish metal trade concession. Jewish participation in trade

with the east is distinctly indicated. It is related
of one R. Abraham b. Hiyyah of Regensburg that
coming from Russia with a heavily laden transport,
he was compelled to stop in Hungary; and of a
Karaitic Commentary of the Pentateuch which,
to the sorrow of a Regensburg rabbi, "was brought
from Babylon to Russia and thence to Regensburg."
A tour of the world undertaken by the Regensburg
Jew Petahiah, in 1180, also reveals the international
communications created by trade interests.

In default of any records of commercial activities
by Augsburg Jews, we are forced to judge by analogy.
It may be taken for granted that the Jews of this
city were not excluded from international trade.

The Regensburg exportations consisted of metal
goods, especially weapons, leather goods (saddles),
textiles and wooden ware. The imports included
principally spices and silks.

It is in the nature of international export trading
that substantial capital must be provided to cover
extended periods. This branch of commerce was
even at that time carried on in large measure
through business associations, or by means of loans,
and there is here another evidence pointing to the
business of Jewish money-lending. Jewish money-
lending, as a special phase of activity, had apparently developed in Augsburg at an earlier period
than at Regensburg. We learn more of Jewish
credit establishments in the former city in former
times than in Regensburg. This may be due to fortuitous lapses in the records, or it may be that the
extended export trade of Regensburg afforded the

Jews a longer and better opportunity to remain
identified with mercantile pursuits.

Actual merchandise trading by Jews died out in
the 13th century. The Lateran Council of 1215 had
again decisively forbidden the charging of interest
by Christians. Decrees enacted by the Rhenish
cities (1255)[24] already indicate the Jews as the
actual money-lenders. It is unlikely that the Jews
of Regensburg and Augsburg should have been
excluded from this general development. Until
about 1400, not only individual Jews, but the Jewish communities of Regensburg and Augsburg were
empowered to affix their own seals to business and
legal documents. At a later day they were compelled, in matters of legal documents—principally
notes of hand—to apply to authorized Christian
officials for the affixing of seals, for which service
payments were duly exacted. In Regensburg the
charges were paid in a lump sum and designated as
"seal and coinage" money. The loss of the seal
privilege indicates a restriction in the right of Jews
to do business.

Until about 1400, members of royal families are
frequently found as debtors of Jews for money
loans. Later, Jewish money-lending activities appear
to have suffered a pronounced recession. The explanation for this may be found in the shrinking of
capital resources suffered by the Jews through the
spoliation policy of King Wenceslaus and the larger
taxes levied by the cities during the wars of the
Swabian Confederation.

The granting of credits to the rulers in Regens-

burg and in Augsburg was, however, as early as
about 1300, conducted to a greater degree by Christians than by Jewish money-lenders. Many noble
and patrician-merchant families had engaged in
this line of business, such as the families Ekker,
Mautner, von Burghausen, Reich, Mäller, etc.
The Jewish money-lenders received interest on
their loans, the Christians received grants of fiscal
privileges carrying political and juridical prefer-
ments. Thus the jurisdiction over Jews was
frequently granted to Christian creditors of the
Bavarian dukes.

The center of gravity of the Jewish money-lending
business in the 14th century could no longer have
been that of commercial credits. Though a number
of such business transactions are doubtless revealed
in the records of that period, they do not appear in
substantial number. The reason for this is to be
found in the fact that at this time the fiscal resources
of the Christian patriciate had been sufficiently
strengthened to enable it to dispense with Jewish
credits. Records of credit given to impoverished
families tend to confirm this conclusion. It is
reasonable to believe, however, that business
transactions on a partnership basis between Christian merchants and Jewish financiers were at times
conducted without any written documents. On
the other hand there are evidences of occasional
secret participation by Christians in the Jewish
money-lending business. In any case if there had
ever existed in Regensburg and Augsburg an
extended credit relation between Jewish banks

and great Christian merchants*, it must have existed before the economic supremacy of the latter, i. e. at a time of which we have hardly any historic records.

In the 13th and 14th centuries ecclesiastical institutions appeared to have had recourse to these Jewish credits; the bishoprics of Augsburg, Regensburg, Freising and numerous monasteries being largely indebted to them. Members of noble and of patrician families residing in the neighborhood of the cities frequently appear as debtors of the Jews. Ecclesiastical institutions and owners of estates in the environs of the city are therefore to be regarded as having been in the 14th century the main customers of the Jewish banks. Alongside and in a measure preceding them, there existed of course the public credit, i. e. voluntary or enforced credits to the government. This was not an established form of credit business, but in spite of this, presented one of the most important problems of Jewish money-lending activities. This was due to the unsystematic financial policy of the later Middle Ages of which we have evidence in Regensburg particularly.

Not until the 15th century is the Jew in Regensburg identified as the provider of credit to the little man, the artisan, the shopkeeper, the priest, the scrivener, the midwife, the innkeeper, in short every vocational phase of the middle class population. The commercial basis for this credit provision was

* There is evidence of such a relation in a limited degree.

the pledge; every kind of garment from the coat-of-mail to the shirt; every utensil, from the chisel to the horse's bridle, is mentioned in the catalogue of pledges. These Regensburg lists date from the end of the 15th century, i. e. from a period in which the impoverished Jews were no longer able to conduct larger credit operations. Is it possible that the Jews might have acted similarly as bankers for the poorer classes at an earlier period? The detailed regulations of the municipal law of Augsburg in 1276 may have reference to this, but the sources divide the money-lending operation into two phases. The one, which proved a menace to the Jews, was the granting of loans to smaller tradespeople, whose impoverished condition compelled them to pledge their last possessions. This was a function exercised by the Jews in their subsequently established public pawnshops. The other phase was the loan of tools to artisans, or of materials to tradespeople, mechanics or manufacturers, for the purpose of creating new means of production. It was, for example, reported by the Jews of Regensburg at the beginning of the 16th century that pieces of iron which had remained unsold had been loaned by them to rural forge-masters in the upper Palatinate. There was therefore in the pawnshop business a stage that lay between the precarious credit of articles of consumption and actual merchandise credit. It must be assumed that in the earlier time, from which the Augsburg municipal law dates, the higher stage of the business held the predominant place, for the reason that the Jewish money-lending activities

played a much more important part in the city's
economy then than it did at a later period.

It becomes evident from this analysis that from
1200 to 1500 we can distinguish various phases of
Jewish credit activities: until 1250, a mercantile
credit to the municipal patriciate, eventually
associated with some form of business partnership;
until about 1400, credits to rulers in need of funds
and to ecclesiastical institutions; after 1400, for
the most part to neighboring nobles and knights,
to artisans and agricultural producers or husbandmen (wine growers, cheese manufacturers, etc.)
within and outside the city. In times of a demand
for public credit—a demand almost uninterrupted
from the period of the first half of the 14th century—there was always the possibility of compelling the Jews to advance credit as though it were
an imposition of taxes.

The Jewish money-lending business, by reason
of its long existence and requirements, had assumed
definitely organized forms. In the larger, especially
the public credit operations, the business was
conducted in the form of an association of several
partners. This was done either as a matter of
necessity, no one individual having sufficient capital,
or perhaps as a precautionary measure, in order to
divide the risks. In more extensive business operations it was found expedient to enlist the participation of Jews from other localities. Thus Jews of
Regensburg had the association of Jews from
Salzburg, Vienna, Prague and Nuremberg. As
Jews frequently changed their domicile, it is diffi-

cult to speak of this matter with accuracy. But this very circumstance favored foreign participation in local money-lending businesses.

The maximum legal interest rate was fixed by the law of the city of Augsburg at 86%. Practically it remained until the end of the Middle Ages at 43 1/3%, a rate already established in 1255 by the Rhenish cities. Variations in these established rates and futile efforts in the direction of further changes have hardly any significance.[25]

It has been maintained, as is well known, that the Jew has a natural penchant for engaging in the business of lending money on interest. The Regensburg and Augsburg historic sources, however, afford no basis for this suggestion. We find there, in the early Middle Ages, as before indicated, a more or less strongly developed trade in commodities, and in the later Middle Ages, by reason of the decline of the money-lending business, a reversion to trade in commodities.[26] Between that beginning and this ending there lay the development of the German guilds, which brought about a far-reaching exclusion of Jews from trade, and the more intensive prohibition of interest by the Church, which enticed the Jews to the money-lending business.

Business activities other than those distinctly commercial were infrequent among the Jews, but were of occasional occurrence. There were of course, for ritualistic reasons, Jewish slaughterers. The established place occupied by the guild of slaughterers was unfavorable to the development of a distinctive Jewish slaughtering industry, and efforts

in this direction were discouraged. Inasmuch as
the Jews bought their bread from Christian bakers,
there do not appear to have been any Jewish bakers.
Here also the antagonistic interests of the guilds are
evidently the only explanation for this. An inadequate number of workers to provide for their daily
needs forced the Jews into contractual arrangements
with Christian slaughterers, potters, etc. In times
of crises Jewish interests were menaced by boycotts
on the part of Christian workers, as when, about
the year 1500, the bakers of Regensburg repeatedly
refused to sell bread to the Jews.[27] There are isolated
appearances of Jewish artisans, viz. needlemakers,
bookbinders, illuminators. There were undoubtedly
in the course of these centuries occasional Jewish
artisans who worked at other handicrafts for distinctively Jewish needs. They cannot be regarded
as having been of importance in the economic condition of the Jewish community, as little as can the
Jewish physicians who made an isolated appearance
from time to time. Significance of a sort may at
most be accorded the physician Abraham, for whom
the anti-Semitic Duke Louis, 1471, procured the
right of domicile in Regensburg.

Restricted and subordinated as was the communal existence of the Jews who were permitted
domicile, so colorful by contrast was the life of the
strolling Jewish apostates. One of these, according
to a confession made in Regensburg about 1475,[28]
had, despite repeated submission to baptism, engaged for several decades in the importation of
etrogim from Greece for the Jews, and had made

journeys that took him from the remotest western to the farthermost southeastern sections of Europe.

Light is thrown by two Regensburg 15th century accounts upon the restricted Jewish communal existence at the end of the Middle Ages. One of these, which has been confirmed by authentic records, tells of the Jewish cantor Kalman who had been so impressed by the "discipline and honor" among the Augustinian monks with whom he had sat at table and who had been so delighted with his experience during a temporary stay at the residence of the suffragan bishop, that he had considered becoming a convert to Christianity. The coarse behavior of the bishop's servants had, however, caused him to change his mind.[29] The other account has its origin in the realm of legend. It reports a magnificent and elaborately decorated residence of a rich Regensburg rabbi of the 15th century.[30] The actual appearance of a Jewish house of the 15th century, and especially of an earlier date, must rather be envisaged as very modest. The insecurity of Jewish existence suppressed any tendencies toward evidences of ostentatious or even comfortable living conditions.

CHAPTER IV

ECONOMIC DEVELOPMENT OF THE JEWS UNTIL THE 19TH CENTURY

During the Middle Ages, the toleration or annihilation of Jews in the German cities was largely dependent upon the favor of the Christian citizenry. The return of the Jews to their former quarters, at a later period, was secured through the favor of the ruling princes. During the period of princely absolutism the cities had suffered a decline in authority.

In Munich, the city in which the Bavarian Elector exercised an arbitrary rule without any constitutional restraint, Jews were denied domicile for longer periods than elsewhere. The strongly Catholic prince opposed the illegal return of Jews which had followed upon the wars and demanded their expulsion.[31] It was not until the middle of the 18th century that a permanently increasing Jewish community is found. This grew out of the financial needs of the rulers for war purposes, costly court entertainments, and the coronation of the Elector as Emperor (1742).

The return of the Jews to Regensburg occurred at a much earlier period. Already in 1543 the Jews had been on the point of obtaining from the Emperor permission for a return to the city, if not as a permanent domicile, at least to come and go daily without restriction for business purposes. The city, remembering at what cost it had succeeded in expelling the Jews, frustrated the plans of the latter for a return.[32] This time again, their return was brought about through the intervention of the leading nobles, namely, the Counts Pappenheim, the hereditary marshals of the realm, whose functions included the supervision of Jewish affairs. In this capacity they had to take care of the Jews, who in connection with the sessions of the Parliament (*Reichstag*) which had been regularly held in Regensburg since 1663, had come to this city in the retinue of other notables. Throughout fully two centuries the conflict between the nobles and the city continued with varying results, the cities frequently making appeals from the counts to their superiors, the Saxon Electors, as the chief marshals of the realm.[33]

The readmittance of the Jews to Augsburg was brought about by similar circumstances; but only temporarily, as for instance in 1714, when the Parliament (*Reichstag*), by reason of the pestilence that raged in Regensburg, was transferred to Augsburg. On this occasion the Counts Pappenheim again assumed the same supervisory attitude in the matter of Jewish affairs. Pressure to accord Jews temporary admittance for business purposes and occasional right of domicile was exerted mainly by the rulers and governmental functionaries.

It was only in Augsburg, however, that the admittance of Jews had a quantitative as well as qualitative significance. For the commercial activities of Munich were too little developed, and Regensburg had never, since its decadence in the later Middle Ages, risen again to greater importance. Furthermore, the Augsburg Jewry of the Middle Ages had survived in a certain sense, even following its dissolution as a commercial organism, since the Jews had been able to maintain their homes in close proximity to the gates of the city. Thus in the newer time the positions of the Regensburg and Augsburg Jews appear to have been reversed. Prior to the Jewish expulsions of the Middle Ages the Jewish community of Regensburg had enjoyed a commercial supremacy, whereas in the battles for resettlement in the 18th century the victory was with Augsburg.

The ultimate readmittance of the Jews into Augsburg was not brought about by the interests of the Christian citizens of this city. On the contrary, it was the interest of the rulers which had to override that of the citizenry. At the same time, the readmission of the Jews is closely identified with the history of the city, and for this reason it is proper in this connection to consider the commercial activities of the Jews that led to this readmission.[34]

CHAPTER V

THE SPIRITUAL DEVELOPMENT

Distinctions are referred to in the Middle Ages between Augsburg and Regensburg Jewish scholarship;[35] between Augsburg and Regensburg peculiarities of ritual; and references are made to the Regensburg pronunciation of Hebrew which differed from the one prevailing in Austria.[36] These variations are, however, few, and hardly discernible in individual cases. The local religious customs (*Minhagim*) were held in reverence by the Jews and were transmitted from generation to generation. But so far as they might serve to provide a clear outline of the cultural existence of the Jews they have no decisive significance. In view of the fact that all the *Minhagim* and their many variants were meticulously observed in those days as a religious duty, it is to be assumed that the peculiarities of the Regensburg and Augsburg ritual practices covered a more extended field than is known to us today, but that only those practices were maintained throughout a longer period which entered into the emotional life for other reasons[37] or possessed a more definite significance by reason of the personal influence of their initiators. Such, for instance, was the use of the spice box (*Gewürz-büchse*) in the *Habdalah*, the introduction of which is traced to a Regensburg rabbi. As the standing and the established influence of the rabbi became greatly diminished in consequence of the growing insecurity of Jewish existence toward the latter part of the 13th century, the local peculiarities must, in the main, be traced to earlier times.

In another sense, however, the spiritual and cultural life of the Regensburg Jews is strongly differentiated from that prevailing in Augsburg. In the former city there was an earlier burgeoning of cultural interests, and these interests continued for a longer period and became comparatively more deeply rooted, paralleling the political-cultural development of both cities.

The Jews of Regensburg dwelt in a city in which the anti-Semitic townsfolk became the dominating factor a century later than they did in Augsburg, in which city they attained supremacy following the uprising of the populace in 1370, whereas in Regensburg this condition ensued only after the popular revolt of 1493.[38] To this was added the fact of the Regensburg Jews' twofold dependence, upon the Crown of Bavaria and the municipality, which had as consequence a conflict of interests between the controlling factions and proved an unintentional advantage to the Jews.[39] These circumstances, in enabling the Jews of Regensburg to maintain their communal existence a hundred years longer than had their coreligionists of Augsburg, promoted, as a matter of course, a greater security in their living conditions and an extension of their interests along cultural lines.

Nay, it seems that the influences exerted by

external conditions manifested themselves not only
in a general cultural development, but also in
individual cases. In consequence of the increasing
insecurity of Jewish living conditions throughout
Southern Germany, since 1250, Jewish cultural
activities had been diverted to Bohemia-Austria
and the neighboring countries, which afforded the
Jews a more tolerant environment. It was not until
the 15th century that there again followed a return,
due to unfavorable conditions developing in Austria
(*Gezerah* of Vienna, 1421). At the same time special
restrictions were encountered by the Jews of Regensburg through the attitude of Duke John *sans pitié*
(i. e. the merciless one), and we do not find in that
city any contemporary Jewish scholars of importance, although there appeared in Augsburg, just at
this time, one of the most distinguished Talmudists
of the later Middle Ages.[40]

The early and, until toward the end of the 14th
century, important commercial activity in Regensburg brought with it not only an early and substantial Jewish incursion to this city, but also a
noteworthy flowering of Jewish culture,[41] paralleling
that of the Rhenish cities and establishing a continued cultural contact with the latter. As was the
case with the higher schools of the Rhenish Jews,
so, too, those of Regensburg were influenced in a
constructive manner by the school of Rabbenu
Tam, the grandson of Rashi, in Northern France.
Even the earliest of the Regensburg Jewish scholars
known to us, Menahem ben Makir (about 1080),
came from the Rhineland, being a native of May-

ence. He was, as were so many of the rabbis of the Middle Ages, a talmudical scholar as well as a religious poet. His *Kinah* "*Ebel a'orer*" is to this day recited at the *tish'ah be-ab* memorial service, as is his *selihah* in the liturgy of the Fast of Esther, "*Adam bekum*".[42] We are familiar with his sixteen *Piyyutim*, four *Selihot* and various religious responsa. He is one of the founders of the Regensburg tradition of scholarship.

At about 1150 there resided and taught in Regensburg, Ephraim ben Isaac, the Old, also designated the "Great", who had spent his early days in France, and is known as the author of *Tosafot* to several talmudic treatises and responsa. His poetical writings, among them four *Zulat*, a *Meorah*, an *Ahabah* and eighteen *Selihot*, resemble in brilliancy of style and grace of expression Spanish examplars, especially Ibn Ezra.[43] The *Selihot* "*Ohel shikken*" and "*Abotai ki bareku*", are to this day in use in the liturgies of the ten Penitential Days (*Busstage*), and also the Fast of the tenth of Tebet, in accordance with the so-called German ritual. He is one of the few German *Tosafists* whose personal characteristics have been credibly transmitted to us. Outstanding in this aspect is his temperamental willfulness. He anathematized those who opposed his religious convictions and did not hesitate in his decisions in religious matters to assert his independent attitude. In this manner he permitted the decorating of synagogues with paintings of animals, in opposition to the decision on this subject of an older Mayence rabbi, and held no religious scruples

against hunting with hounds and falcons, providing
that this practice involved no tormenting of animals.
His influence is clear when we find a later writer
admitting the literal permissibility of the practice,
but adding, in a manner characteristic of the Jewish
attitude to this outstanding diversion of the German people, the well known saying of the Rabbis
that in the enjoyment of the "flesh of the Levia-
than", i. e. in the heavenly bliss, the hunter will
not be allowed to participate. It was this same
Rabbi Ephraim who is said to have introduced the
use of the Spice Box (*Besamim-Büchse*) at the
Habdalah.[44]

Another prominent figure is a younger contemporary of this Rabbi Ephraim, by the name of
Petahiah ben Jacob. He was a brother of the
Tasafist, Isaac "the Wise", of Prague. Nothing is
known of the circumstances of his life, not even
whether he was a man of scholarly attainments,
nor whether he resided for any length of time in
Regensburg or in Prague—both of which cities
were associated in intimate commercial relations—[45]
nor what had impelled him to undertake his extended
journey to the Orient, an account of which, edited
at a later period, is given in the writing, *Sibub
ha-'Olam*, i. e. "Around the World". The road
taken by this traveler led from Prague and Poland
and the Crimea, to Bagdad and Persia, and back
across Palestine and Greece. It is not credible
that—as has been conjectured—the travels of
Benjamin of Tudela brought about this *Sibub* as
a competitive undertaking, or that a visit to the

heads of the academies in Babylonia had been the
incentive to these travels. It is much more probable
that the impetus was due to curiosity (*Neugier*),
as is asserted by the past-master of modern Jewish
culture.[46]   In fact such a journey, in view of the
many trips to the Orient undertaken for commercial
purposes and not infrequently by Jewish merchants
of Prague and Regensburg, is nothing very remarkable. The memoranda of Petahiah's travels are
said to have been collected and edited by Judah he-
Hasid.

There was still another Regensburg rabbi of
that time who is reported to have undertaken a
journey to Palestine: this was Baruk ben Isaac,
doubtless identical with the author of the *halakic*
compilation, *Sefer ha-Terumah*. This writer was
resident in Regensburg in 1200, as was his contemporary, Judah he-Hasid (died about 1217), who
ranks as one of the most remarkable personalities
among the German Jews of the Middle Ages. He
may have come to Regensburg about 1195 after
having spent his early days in Speyer, of which we
have some characteristic accounts. The report
may be legendary that at the age of eighteen
he had manifested no interest in cultural matters
and passed his time in the practice of archery.
Stories of this sort are also told about such
illustrious scholars as R. Akiba, Maimonides
and others, in order to satisfy the need for
contrast. This legend, even if not literally
accepted, may have its significance if we consider
the later manifestations of his life-work with

their pronounced emotional and imaginative tendencies, for it reveals the unaffected phases of his character, which are also discernible in his teachings.

Similarly pronounced characteristics are reported of his father, Samuel the Pious, of Speyer (born about 1115). He, too, had deviated from the prevailing conceptions and methods of a purely philosophic-juridical approach to the study and interpretation of the Talmud, and became the representative of a mystical tendency of thought among the Jews of Germany. This tendency was most intensively crystallized in its requirement of a profound devotion in the act of prayer; in the mystical interpretation of devotional texts, especially in the utilization of the numerical values of the Hebrew letters (*Gematria*), and, finally, in the independent attitude of the devotee in relation to the text and terminology of the prayer. The latter had to be, before all else, comprehended by the devotee. This idea, closely identified with many similar Jewish and non-Jewish manifestations in all periods, finds expression also in the content of the individual prayers composed by the two "Pious" (*Fromme*), Samuel, the father, and Judah, the son, notably also in the still read *Shir ha-Yihud* (Hymn of Unity) and *Shir ha-Kabod* (Hymn of Honor), both of which are attributed to these writers. The son is recognized as the actual author of the subsequently developed and frequently elaborated *Sefer Hasidim*, i. e. "Book of the Pious". The father, however, is credited with a substantial participation in the composition and formulation of this work. The word *Hasid* connotes as a surname, as does its corresponding German expression, *fromm* (pious), a special reference to the devotion of the heart in a mystical sense, and in the medieval spirit it was associated with the idea of being "initiated into the mysteries", and, on the basis of this knowledge, qualified to perform miracles, corresponding to the German term *vielwissend*. This was a personal phase of religiosity, and was held in high esteem, without at first provoking any conflict with the otherwise prevailing rational theological concepts, the less so as these two original *Hasidim* were recognized as Talmudists. This association of an esteemed, though exclusive, scholarship with a popular "piety" in the sense mentioned was the basis of the great reputation enjoyed by Judah the Pious, as well as by his *Book of the Pious*, which even until most recent times has made its appearance in ever new editions. This recognition finds expression in the words coined in his honor by posterity: "In the days of the prophets he would have been a prophet; in the days of the teachers of the Law he would have been a teacher of the Law"— a tribute that places him in the ranks of those who were held in highest honor and esteem by the authorities of the older Jewish tradition. Upon this recognition rested the widespread and profound influence exerted by Judah the Pious as Rabbi of Regensburg. It was in his time that a reorganization of the local Jewish community took place, which acquired, in 1210, a new burial terrain and

the site for a new synagogue structure, which had
a seating capacity of about 300 and was designed
in the style of early Gothic architecture. It continued to be for nearly 300 years the house of prayer
for the Jews, until it was converted, following the
Jewish expulsion of 1519, into a chapel of the Virgin
Mary (today the New Protestant Parish Church).[47]
The painter, Altdorfer, made an etching of this
synagogue shortly before its demolition. There are
no known *halakic* writings by Judah the Pious.
The comparatively subordinate estimation in which
the mere study of the Talmud was held by him is
disclosed if we compare the prevailing school cur-
riculum in his day with his Regulation: "If your
son is making progress in his biblical studies, but
not in the Talmud, then the study of the latter may
be deferred until he reaches the age of sixteen.
If, however, he is even then not equal to this study,
he should be directed to the reading of an abridged
Talmud and the midrashic literature (i. e. homi-
letic interpretations)." All the known writings of
Judah—the greater part is lost—are concerned
with mystical interpretations of the prayers and
the Bible and with moral precepts. Significant and
in part of high cultural and historical value are
the following excerpts from his writings:[48]

(1) *Of a Pious Life:*

"Even the most devout can make no claim to
a heavenly reward; nor can he requite even the
least of the many kindnesses with which God has
favored him. Serve God therefore out of pure

love, and not in the expectation of Paradise. Sacrifice your life for God, so that you may not be lower than the hirelings who at the command of mortals give up their lives in battle. We must submit ourselves to pain and suffering that our soul may become perfect. We should never deny that we are Jews.

"Do not say: I will punish the evil one, but hope for God's help. If one has deceived or despoiled or maligned you, do not requite it with a similar misdeed. If one reviles you, hold your peace and prevail upon your household to do likewise. If one has placed unrighteous imposts upon you, while those who are richer than you are made to pay less, do not provoke a quarrel by contending, but hold your peace, and devote yourself to sacred learning. Do not permit yourself to cavil at the good fortune of the wicked, for their end will be disastrous. Ill goeth it at times with the good so that one may not believe him to be good only in the days of good fortune. If the leaders of a congregation are unworthy, this is a punishment for its failure to appreciate worthy leaders. The children of righteous proselytes are to be preferred in marriage for your children to those of dishonest Jews.

"Act honorably toward everyone, and be not contentious in your relations with either Jews or non-Jews. Be upright in business. Do not say that one has offered you this or that price for

your wares if this be not the truth. If you do not
wish to dispose of your goods do not pretend
that you desire to sell them. If a Jew or a non-
Jew desires to borrow from you, and you do not
wish to make the loan, do not say that you have
not the money, if this should not be the truth.
The money of those who clip coin, practice usury,
weigh and measure dishonestly, carries no blessing. Their children and their assistants will become outcasts and beggars.

"The greatest defect is thanklessness, even
against animals. He also is deserving of punishment who overloads the beast of burden beyond
its strength, or beats it; who pulls the ears of
cats, or digs spurs into the flesh of horses. If
you have slaves and must dispose of them, do
not sell them to those who are cruel and who
treat them inhumanly.

"Do not spit when you encounter the leprous,
for they are as truly God's creatures as those
that are sound.

"There is no blessing in the wealth of those
who oppress their laborers, or are the purchasers
of stolen goods, or who include pagan ornaments
among the utensils of their homes. They or
their children will suffer the loss of all their
possessions."

(2) *Of Our Relations to our Fellowmen*:

"He who is himself compassionate toward his
fellows, with him will God be compassionate.
He who is without mercy resembles the beast,

who remains unconcerned at the sufferings of its kind. Many will suffer poverty because they have treated the poor with disdain or have said that they would not give assistance to those who are able to work. One should rather give to the poor that which he wastes upon useless things, such as the birds in his possession.

"The sons of parents who make use of counterfeit coins or false weights will follow in their footsteps. In most instances, wicked parents will have wicked children. Cupidity in connection with marriage contracts leads to the dissolution of piety. A poor man refused to marry a rich woman because her brothers were not reputable men. While it is not forbidden to contract a marital alliance with such a woman, there are many things that are not prohibited, the commission of which, must, however, eventually be answered for.

"Mistrust one who speaks evil of your enemy, and him who sings the praise of one who could bring him advantage. If one keeps his affairs a secret from you, trust him not. Do not confide that to your friend which you would not have known to your enemy, unless it be that you have often had occasion to prove his fidelity. Do not betray to others what has been told you in confidence. Before you speak you are the master of your word, after you have uttered it, your word becomes your master. If you behold persons

whispering to one another, do not ask them to
reveal their secret to you, so that they may not
be induced to speak falsehood.

"If you would know what are the thoughts of
people, place books before them, and the choice
that they make will reveal the trend of their
thoughts. Money given to provide garments for
the poor is more properly expended than to
inscribe scrolls of the Torah. But the noblest
charity is to provide work for the poor, even
though one is not in need of their labor.

"If you associate with non-Jews, bestir yourself to deal with them as honestly as you would
in your transactions with Jews. Call the attention of the non-Jew to any error. It is better for
you to subsist upon alms than that you appropriate the money of strangers and bring discredit
upon the Jewish name. Hold in higher honor the
righteous non-Jew than a Jew who neglects the
divine commands. On the whole, the habits and
morals of Jews and non-Jews are the same in
most places."

(3) *Of Reactions to Jewish Persecutions:*

"When you speak in the night, moderate your
voice. When you speak in the day, take heed of
the wall behind you, for if your foot stumble, the
hurt can be remedied, but should your tongue
stumble, it may cost you your life.

"Should the enemy say: Deliver up to us one
of your people that we may put him to death,
otherwise we will destroy all of you,—then let

them destroy all. Should they say: Deliver a woman to us that we may dishonor her, otherwise we will dishonor all of your women,—then let them dishonor all.

"In a certain city the Jews were given the alternative of abjuring their religion or of being put to death, and the rabbi permitted all of them to submit to baptism, if they would later return to the Jewish fold. All followed his advice, but in the end the rabbi will be made answerable for having led them into sin."

(4) *Of Popular Superstition:*

"If one should offer you an amulet as being helpful in acquiring favor or riches, do not accept it, but place your trust wholly in God.

"The injunction 'Love thy neighbour' also implies that one should not withhold from his neighbor a helpful amulet. The inscribing of adjurations and similar incantations should be avoided, as harm might befall some one who utilizes them.

"There was one who fell asleep in the House of God, and when he awoke at midnight he beheld the spirits of the departed in their prayer shawls, and among them two living persons. These two died shortly thereafter.

"Divination is a most sinful practice, but is today frequent in Israel. One should not expect the arrival of a guest when a flame leaps up, or that a traveler will fall into the water if one pours water into the fire. Also one should not wait

until the appearance of the new moon to begin
the instruction of children, for even the choice
of special days is idolatrous. Even though superstitious practices are forbidden, there exist various dependable omens, but it is better that one
does not speak of them, so that others may not
be led into superstition. Thus itching of the foot
foretells the approach to a strange place; of the
ears, that one is to hear news; in the eyes, that
something new is to be seen or read; in the hand,
that one is to receive money,—whereby God
gives indications to mankind of coming events,
through their physical members.

"Only those become the victims of demons who
provoke them through the use of amulets, invo-
cations and similar practices. They hold no
wisdom and they shorten one's life. It is best
that man should make his prayer to God that He
guard him from all evil. The names of the angels
are not mentioned in the Holy Scriptures, in
order that they be not used for purposes of invo-
cation. Who concerns himself with such matters
will come to a bad end. Many who have resorted
to such practices have met with disaster; they
have become baptized or have fallen into sick-
ness. Even when one undertakes a journey one
should not invoke the angels, but should make
one's prayers to God.

"One should not bathe in a stream that has
been used for trial by ordeal, as it has served a
heathenish use.

"When the assassin approaches his victim the

wound begins to bleed. Since that happens also upon the approach of one who has eaten soup without bread, one should, to avoid suspicion, eat dry bread with one's soup.

"It has happened that a child has been born with teeth and a tail. It was to have been put to death, that it might not grow up to be a cannibal; but it was ordered by the rabbi that its teeth be extracted and the tail cut off, that it might become harmless.

"A woman was suspected of having devoured children, and it was decided to put her to death. The rabbi, however, prevented this, inasmuch as the Jews possessed no capital jurisdiction, and the woman, obsessed by sinister powers, was innocent; and it was ordered that it be announced in the synagogue, in her presence, that if a child should again come to grief, all the women should whet their teeth on the stone coping of the well, which would bring about the death of the guilty ones.

"A child cried in the night, and it became known that it had been bewitched by a Jewish woman. The mother went to the rabbi and declared that she could heal her child, but that its ailment would then be transferred to the child of the witch who had caused the affliction. The rabbi then forbade the healing, with the words: 'If the mother be guilty, what wrong has the child committed?'

"Drops of blood are found, at times, upon certain trees. One should not fell such trees in order not to provoke the demons."

All these pronouncements are rather character-istic of the spirit of the times than representative of the personal opinions of Judah he-Hasid, for it is not known to what an extent later interpolations may have been made in these writings. It is inter-esting in this connection to note the wisdom that frequently characterized the decisions made by the rabbis to whom such questions were submitted, and whose purpose it was to make harmless the superstitions of the populace, without actually impugning their validity. In both phases, namely the prevalence of superstitious beliefs and the critical judgment applied to them, the Jewish and the Christian attitude of those days were closely related, and the same judgment of Judah he-Hasid is revealed by his teaching, in a period of intensive Jewish persecutions, that "in most places the Jews and Christians resemble one another in their ethical and moral concepts of life".

With the 13th century the scholarly tradition died out in Regensburg, experiencing a faint revival in the 15th century. This extinction was apparently due to the migration of the scholars to Bohemia and Austria, in which countries the absolutism of the princes and their favor enjoyed by the Jews proved of advantage to them until the 15th century. This was notably the case in the time of the "Inter-regnum" (1254–1273), when the precarious condi-tion of Jewish existence in western Germany was at its height, and Jews began to migrate in large numbers to eastern localities. There was a slight reaction after 1400, following a turn for the worse

in Bohemia, due to the predatory policy of King
Wenceslaus and to the occurrences in Austria that
reached their peak in the Vienna "*Gezerah*" of 1421.

In the middle of the 13th century, there is found,
however, a faint echo of Jewish scholarship in
Regensburg. There resided temporarily in this city
the renowned Isaac Or Zaru'a (about 1180–1260),
a pupil of Judah he-Hasid; and the "eccentric
literalist" (*wunderliche Buchstabengläubige*)—so
designated by Graetz—Moses Taku (i. e. of
Tachau?), who simultaneously attacked the rational-
ism of the Maimonists and the rising Cabala. These
two also resided in Austria throughout the greater
part of their lives. The older scholarly tradition
survives, however, in the legend that Asher ben
Jehiel (about 1250–1327) is buried in Regensburg,
and in the widespread reverence in which the
Regensburg burial ground was held till the end of
the Middle Ages as the sepulcher of many *Zad-
dikim*.[49] For a short time, too, Maharil (R. Jacob
ha-Levi, about 1355–1427) is said to have officiated
in Regensburg as rabbi and cantor. He was one
of the illustrious Jewish scholars of his day. A
larger number of Jewish scholars in Regensburg
appear again in the 15th century, but their work
was not of special importance. It was a period in
which preoccupation with Jewish studies was hamp-
ered by the "continued fears and persecutions" to
which the Jews were subjected.[50] As authorities in
talmudic learning appear the names of Simon ha-
Levi, Benjamin Katz, Moses Mendel and Jonah,
son of the Viennese Rabbi Shalom. In the same

period a Regensburg Jew named Liwa translated the Book of Samuel into German.[51] Significant of the condition of the Jews of that day is the vagrant existence of the most important among the later Regensburg scholars of the 15th century, Rabbi Israel ben Hayyim of Brünn (about 1410–1480). His life was so checkered and eventful that it has formed in recent days a subject for dramatic representation.[52] He was a pupil of Jacob Weil of Erfurt (see below, p. 69) and of Israel Isserlein of Vienna-Neustadt. His coming to Regensburg was probably occasioned by the expulsion of the Jews from Brünn (1454),[53] but he may, perhaps, have come at an earlier date, establishing a school in this city in the face of violent opposition. Rabbi Amshel, the incumbent of the Regensburg rabbinate, opposed his right to perform rabbinical functions, the contention giving rise to considerable disturbance in the community. It is not unlikely that the later reference made by the converted Jew, Antonius Margherita (see below, p. 69), to the effect that the contemporary expulsion of the Jews from Regensburg had been precipitated by their internal dissensions, was based upon these disturbances. Despite the fact that the two above mentioned teachers of Israel b. Hayyim, as well as other authorities, took his part in this contention, he was subjected to much distress. His discourses were interrupted, his seat in the synagogue was defaced with crucifixes, regarded as the symbol of extreme revilement, and he was violently denounced by the authorities. That he was regarded, despite these animadversions, as the spiritual head of the community, is indicated by the fact that he was placed under arrest in order to force the Jews to pay for the "defence against the Turks" (*Türkenhilfe*), i. e. the extraordinary imposts levied in the war with Turkey. He was again, shortly thereafter, taken into custody, upon the charge made by a converted Jew that he had been supposedly concerned in the purchase of a Christian child (1474). On the eve of his subjection to the torture on this charge, he was, upon the insistent intervention of the Emperor and the King of Bohemia, released from custody and his calumniator was condemned to death in his place after having withdrawn his accusation.[54] Rabbi Israel's Responsa achieved a high reputation. Characteristic of these times of troubled existence is the supreme importance attached to the efforts made by him and by his contemporaries at safeguarding the rabbinical office from "degeneration and degradation,"[55] a danger that affected the Jewish no less than the Christian clergy in those days before the "church reformation". His life is interwoven with the death-struggle of the Regensburg Jewish community of the Middle Ages, and only for the reason that this struggle dragged itself through several decades,[56] owing to political involvements, did he have any successors in the Regensburg rabbinate. One of these was Rabbi Isaac Stein, also called Eisik Levi, of whom little is known. Another was the Jacob Margolis to whom Johannes Reuchlin turned for information regarding cabalistic literature, and whose Christian son,

Antonius Margherita, was the author of the work,
Der ganze jüdische Glaub (The Entire Jewish Faith,
Augsburg, 1530), which writing is charged with
having been one of the causes of turning Luther to
bitter animosity against the Jews.

With the expulsion of the Jews from Regensburg
in 1519, the thread of the Middle Age development
is torn asunder. It may be worth noting that in
the 17th century a Christian writer refers depre-
catingly to the fact that Solomon Zevi, the author
of *Der jüdische Theriak* (Hanau, 1615), was abandoned by his coreligionists and died miserably in
Regensburg.[57]

The earliest representatives of Jewish culture in
Augsburg made their first appearance when, in the
last days of the 13th century, Jewish scholarship in
Germany entered upon its decline. Mention is made
by a Jewish writer, shortly thereafter, of a Rabbi
Hayyim Augsburg, of whom no date is given.[58]
Elias of Augsburg was one of the commentators of
the *Semag* (*Sefer Mizvot Gadol*) by Moses of Coucy.
Among the victims of 1349 appears the name of
Rabbi Senior. From Höchstadt, a township in the
vicinity of Augsburg, came Joseph ben Moses (about
1420–1490), known mainly through the title of his
book *Leket Yosher*. This work contains important
source material for medieval Jewish history. He
was a pupil of Jacob Weil and Israel Isserlein, to
whom further reference will be made in the following pages. His tribulations, like those experienced
by many of his contemporaries, testify to the
disturbed conditions that affected many Jewish

scholars of the time. His destiny led him to Italy,
where he functioned as rabbi in Mestre, Padua and
Cremona. His teacher, Jacob Weil, was the most
famous of the Augsburg rabbis of the Middle Ages.
He officiated as rabbi at the time of the expulsion
of the Jews from Augsburg (1438) and migrated at
that time to Bamberg and later to Erfurt. He was
a pupil of Maharil. Among his personal characteristics his devotion to the cause of peace was widely
recognized. In Nuremberg he is said to have been
subjected, in connection with questions of jurisdiction, to difficulties similar to those experienced at
a later date by Israel of Brünn, in Regensburg (see
above), but through his voluntary renunciations,
he avoided every contention.[59] In his Responsa
there is also revealed his effort, in contrast to the
prevailing casuistry of the *Pilpul*, to base his decisions upon clear proof rather than upon hair-
splitting disputations (*Dikduk*).[60] He manifested
a keenly critical attitude toward the lack of learning on the part of many who posed and functioned
as rabbis, and inveighed against their corrupt practices. The most enduring of his contributions is his
collection of regulations regarding *Shehitah*, which
are observed to this day and have been continually
republished. Following the Jewish expulsion from
Augsburg (1438), with which Jacob Weil was contemporary, the *Hakmé Pfersee*, may be regarded
as the incumbents of the former Augsburg rabbinate.
Pfersee was one of the near lying towns which did
not come under the Augsburg municipal control,
and which afforded a place of refuge for the Jews

until the time of the Emancipation. Known by
name among these congregational leaders was Rabbi
Liebermann, a friend of Joselmann of Rosheim
(about 1530), and Rabbi Enoch Sundel, author of
the *Reshit Bikkurim*, who fled from Poland in 1648,
and after a temporary stay in Prague and Oettingen,
migrated to Pfersee. In 1680, his son, Judah Löb,
succeeded him in the rabbinate. His successors
were Judah Löb ben Issachar Bär Oppenheimer
(*Minhat Yehudah*) with his Dayyan, Isaac Etten-
hausen (*Or Ne'elam*), and later, Benjamin Wolf
Spira, of Prague. The latter died in 1792.

The Augsburg rabbis from the 16th to the threshold of the 19th century came almost without exception from Eastern Europe, the reservoir of talmudic
learning in those days. The so-called *Pfersee Talmud*
is one of the treasures in the State Library of
Munich.[61] The reference to this valuable collection
of Jewish writings invites a brief examination of
those Christian coteries of Regensburg and Augsburg whose interests were directed to Jewish studies
during the "Humanistic" period. We have already
referred above to the correspondence between the
Swabian Johannes Reuchlin and the Regensburg
Rabbi, Jacob Margolis. Many Hebrew books were
printed in Augsburg under Christian auspices between 1514 and 1543. The town-clerk of Augsburg,
Conrad Peutinger (1465–1547), who was a collector
of Jewish antiquities, was, in view of his official
position, identified with Jewish political matters.
His attitude in this regard was unfriendly to the
Jews. He was primarily interested in ancient Jewish

tombstones, quite a number of which had been preserved from the time of the medieval Jewish expulsions with their attendant demolition of burial grounds, and had been kept as memorials in public places. Their use also as building material in the construction of public and private edifices had attracted the attention of collectors. Fantastic statements were made at that time regarding their antiquity, which receive credence to this day. Peutinger, too, was looking especially for tombstones of Roman times, and there was a constant inclination to ascribe the most remote dates to tombstones and monuments unless a later date was quite certain. The tombstone of a Roman soldier, Kleophas, in the Augsburg museum is sometimes erroneously regarded even now as that of a Jewish legionary.[62] What was a phase of scholarship among the Christian classicists, was for the Jews a pious reverence of their ancestors, and at the time of their expulsion they requested that their old burial places remain intact, and pledged themselves to defray the cost of maintaining them, without, however, any practical result.

Humanistic interests also influenced the first attempts of the Jews to return to Regensburg and Augsburg in the course of the 18th century. There was then, too, an intensified revival of interest in Jewish matters on the part of Christian scholars. The famous Chronicler of Regensburg, C. Th. Gemeiner, manifested the liveliest interest in the history of the Jews of his native city. Again and again the interests and investigations of scholars

were directed to ancient Jewish tombstones and
monuments which were scattered throughout the
land as far as the Austrian territory. Fantastic
conjectures followed the discovery of underground
passages beneath the former Jewish quarters which
were being uncovered in the course of excavations.
Christian scholarship alone, however, was not the
determining factor in this awakened interest in
Jewish matters, an impelling motive lying in the
new world-outlook and the political discussions pro-
jected by the question of Jewish emancipation.
Similar influences affected the new tendency toward
a secular culture among the Jews. Already in 1750
one of the wealthy Augsburg Jews had taken a
Christian teacher of the German language into his
home. It was not only an intensive interest in
intellectual culture that expressed itself in these
matters, but a requirement associated with the
practical affairs of life, the Jews having latterly
gained prominence in public interests as war-
contractors and Court Factors, and it became
incumbent upon them to identify themselves with
the current of world affairs.

Even the first community rabbi of Regensburg,
in the newer time, (Eisik) Isaac Alexander (1722–
1802), gave the predominant place in his interests
to the fostering of secular culture. He had in his
day achieved some recognition through his literary
works, but was not long remembered. His intellectual tendencies are indicated in the titles of his
writings: *Vereinigung des mosaischen Gesetzes mit
dem Talmud* (Unity of the Mosaic Law with

the Talmud), *Von der Freiheit des Menschen* (Of
Human Freedom), *Von dem Dasein Gottes* (Of the
Existence of God), *Die selbstredende Vernunft* (Clear
Reason), *Wahrheiten zur göttlichen Weisheit* (Per-
ceptions of Divine Wisdom), *Salomo und Josef II*
(Solomon and Joseph II). He translated into German the *Shir ha-Yihud* (Song of Unity), from the
Liturgy. He was related in his spiritual tendencies
to his contemporary, Moses Mendelssohn, without
approaching the latter's intellectual scope. A cor-
rect characterization of him is supplied by Friedrich
Nicolai, who had occasion to become acquainted
with him, and refers to him as the author "of various
German writings, which, though they are imbued
with a somewhat alien oriental coloring, contain
matters of merit and of especial value to his
people".[63]

A modest booklet by the Regensburg merchant,
Maier Löw, *Anleitung zur Erlernung der heiligen
hebräischen Sprache* (Introduction to the Study of
the Sacred Hebrew Language, 1788), provides an
attempt to reconcile Jewish-Christian intellectual
interests, although with a somewhat different tendency. It is intended for the guidance of Christians,
and is dedicated to the Bishop of Regensburg.

Following the death of Isaac Alexander, the
Regensburg rabbinate was taken over by Jacob
Seligmann (1757–1833). He took the name of Jacob
Weil in obedience to the governmental ordinance
commanding the adoption of permanent Jewish
surnames. At the same time the Regensburg cantor,
later Rabbi, Mendel Joseph (1770–1849), adopted

the fanciful name Emanuel Sonnentheil. Then, too,
the foremost Jewish physician in Regensburg won
for himself title and distinction as: the Bavarian
Councilor and Army Physician, Dr. M. Cannstadt.
He was born in Erlangen and came to Regensburg
in 1831, where he won distinction in connection with
his treatment of cholera, for the further study of
which he went to Paris in 1832. He was subsequently appointed director of the Cholera Hospital
in Brussels. While Professor at the University of
Erlangen, after 1844, he published his *Annual
Reports of the Progress of Medicine*, an important
technical journal, the publication of which was
subsequently continued by the renowned clinician,
R. von Virchow.

Under the rabbinate of Jacob Weil, a Jewish
burial ground was established in 1822,[64] and, in
1832, a Jewish school was instituted. Dr. Seligmann
Schlenker was called from Fürth to act as director
of the latter (1800–1860). But it was just this man
who emphasized the fact that the Jewish cultural
problem had become a distinctly controversial one.
When in 1832 his application for the rabbinical post
was refused by the congregation on the ground of
deficient scholarship in Judaica, he turned to the
Bavarian governmental authorities, who had reserved for themselves the right of confirmation,
with the claim that philosophic culture and moral
instruction were of greater importance than acquaintance with and cultivation of ancient Jewish
literature. It was finally agreed that the rabbinate
be conducted jointly by Sonnentheil and Schlenker.

Following the death of the former (1849), the rabbinate was taken over by Schlenker alone. He had no further difficulties because the Revolution of 1848 transferred the greater part of the Jewish spiritual energies to the liberal assimilationists. Following Schlenker's death, in 1860, the Regensburg Jewish community remained for an extended period subordinate to the neighboring Sulzbürg rabbinate, until 1882, when a rabbi of the older Jewish tendency became its spiritual leader, Dr. Seligmann Meyer, who was also active as a publicist. Dr. Magnus Weinberg, formerly the rabbi of Sulzbürg, who has been in office since 1929, has done creditable research work in history.

In 1903, the distinguished musical authority, Abraham Zevi Idelsohn, was called to Regensburg as Cantor, retaining this post for several years, until he migrated to Jerusalem in 1906. He became Professor of Jewish Music at the Hebrew Union College in Cincinnati, Ohio, retiring in 1934. He died in 1938.

The more recent Jewish community of Augsburg is, as was the medieval congregation of this city, younger than that existing in Regensburg. The Jewish community of Augsburg was not accorded a legalized civic recognition until 1861. Dr. Jacob Hirschfeld was called to its rabbinate from Fünfkirchen in Hungary. He functioned until 1875, and was one of the delegates to the Leipzig Rabbinical Conference of 1871.[65] His successor, Heinrich Gross, also a native of Hungary, was a prominent historian. His *Gallia Judaica*, the material for which he had assembled in Paris while a tutor in the household of Baron Günzburg, still holds an important place as a valuable scientific work for students. The not infrequent selection of eastern Jewish rabbis by German Jewish congregations was significant for the intellectual situation of these Jewries. Specific Jewish culture had suffered decadence in Germany. The members of Jewish congregations had grown continually more liberal-minded along cultural lines, though they acquiesced at first as a matter of loyalty in maintaining the traditional forms in their religious services.

A change occurred in this attitude when, in 1910, the Augsburg rabbinate was occupied by Dr. Heinrich Grünfeld, another German-born Jew. He introduced, with some modifications, the Reform Prayer Book of Leopold Stein. His little book, *Brief Survey of the History of the Jews of Augsburg*, appeared in 1912 as a festive publication in connection with the dedication of the beautiful new synagogue, whose designer and builder was the Jewish architect, Fritz Landauer, of Munich. His successor was a German liberal rabbi, Dr. Ernst Jacob, who has won some fame through his historical-religious works, especially his *Israelitische Religionslehre* (Israelitic Religious Teaching) for use in religious schools.

On the whole, the intellectual life of the cities of Augsburg and Regensburg suffered a decline throughout the 19th century,—and this not only so far as the Jews were concerned,—by reason of the close proximity of the city of Munich, which, in its quality of being the seat of government and

ranking as a university town, a theatrical center
and a metropolis of art, exerted a powerful cultural
influence and held a far-reaching attraction. There
was concentrated in Munich every phase of Jewish
cultural productiveness, and the formerly more
important cities of Augsburg and Regensburg were
wholly overshadowed by Munich in the 19th
century.

A description of Jewish cultural existence in the
capital and university city of Munich would in
itself form a work of considerable scope. In the
course of the 19th century, Munich had developed
into an art center of world-wide renown. Its library
was one of the largest in Germany, and contained
rare treasures, including Hebrew manuscripts and
printed works. The city grew to be a center of
attraction of the first rank for persons interested in
cultural attainments, Jews no less than Christians.
It maintained this attraction from the Munich
days of Heinrich Heine to the time of the resigna-
tion of Richard Willstätter from the Professorship
of Chemistry at the University, in which a continually increasing anti-Semitic spirit was being manifested.

But scant reference can be given here to the large
number of Jews who, contributing to and enjoying
the cultural opportunities of the city, held temporary
residence in Munich without associating themselves
with specifically Jewish spiritual or cultural interests.
We must, however, speak of them, not because
Jews had exerted any characteristic influence upon
the city's cultural atmosphere—manifested here to

a lesser degree than perhaps in Berlin or in Frankfort-on-the-Main—but rather because the light-
hearted gaiety that characterized this city of big
carnival festivities attracted vagabond Jewish
elements and developed them in this direction.
When, after 1880, anti-Semitism spread in intensified form throughout all of Germany, there continued in the Catholic, self-assertive city of Munich
a sort of unwilling tolerance that bore an illusory
resemblance to a liberalistic spirit. This atmosphere
proved distinctly favorable to the development of
an independent literary and artistic activity,
especially in Jewish circles.

Heinrich Heine had already recognized the fasci-
nation of the *genius loci*, and had spent some time
in Munich as editor of a local periodical. Resembling
him, though in many points entirely different, was
a native of Munich, Friedrich Julius Stahl (1802–
61), whose name had been Jolson before his baptism
in early youth. He resembled Heine in his inexorable, his ruthless and unyielding intellectual keen-
ness. He differed from him in his equally inexorable
aversion from Judaism, which made it possible
for him to become "entirely Christian and Prussian",
and to receive in Berlin appointment as instructor
of the Prussian nobility and as a political leader of
the Prussian Conservative Party. His convictions
were bound to provoke in him a determined opposition to a complete Jewish emancipation. A course
of life such as Stahl's, is fundamentally determined
by personal characteristics. There can be no doubt,
however, that the young Jolson felt himself more

directly attracted by the scholarly culture that had
been expounded to him in Munich by Thiersch
and Weiler than by the Jewish studies that had
been imparted to him in the home of his grand-
father, Abraham Uhlfelder.   This indicates the
cultural situation in the two camps.

The inferior status of Jewish cultural life at the
beginning of the 19th century changed in the course
of time to the advantage of the Jews. It is true
that later also there was a secession from Judaism
on the part of intellectual personalities of note,
such as the Director General of Music in Munich,
Herman Levi (born in Giessen, 1839; died in
Munich, 1900), who had conducted the first per-
formance of Richard Wagner's *Parsifal* in 1882.
But there was absent in the later period that
positive inclination toward Christianity which had
so completely filled and swayed the life of Stahl.
It may be possible to discern a somewhat similar
attitude in a less significant intellectual sphere as
represented by Paul Nicolaus Cosmann.   Born
about 1870, he attracted attention as publisher
of the widely read *Süddeutsche Monatshefte* (South
German Monthly), and became about 1922 one of
the principal contributors to the well known anti-
Semitic daily, *Muenchner Neueste Nachrichten*,
without, however, producing anything comparable
to his former work.

A fourth personality, very much indebted to the
cultural life of Munich, is the contemporary popular
writer Lion Feuchtwanger, a belated product of
the old Munich culture. He was born in 1884, the

scion of an observant Jewish family, and grew
to manhood in the period of the florescence of
the Munich vaudeville. The thoroughly sceptical
and untrammeled spirit revealed in his subject-
matter and composition, together with a high order
of wit and a talent for graphic presentation, give
proof of his origins in the Munich of 1900, though
they show at the same time the cosmopolitan
spirit of the Jew of the metropolis.

In contrast to the native son of Munich to whom
we have just referred, there was Gustav Landauer,
whose fate led him to choose Munich as his home.
Born in Karlsruhe in 1870, he met a violent death
in Munich in 1919, a victim of the political conflicts
in which he had participated. He had striven for
the establishment of a socialistic community based
upon the principle of human brotherhood, but far
removed from the economic theory of materialistic
Marxism. It was his belief that the hour had
struck for the establishment of such a Republic,
and that the opportunity for its realization would
be lost if he, the Jew, failed to give his aid to the
undertaking in the capital city of Bavaria. It was
an error of judgment at once characteristic of the
fine litterateur deficient in a knowledge of world
affairs and of the Jew in his cosmopolitan outlook
on life. Landauer's earnest but unbalanced existence, the interests of which hovered between
playwriting, political literature, practical political
experimentation and historical writings, could
only have found a stage for its activities, if any-
where, in a metropolitan city, such as the Munich

of that time, where there was an outlet for every
idea and where everything met with a friendly
reception. A characteristic phase of the cultural
life of Munich was also the relatively large number
of Jewish antiquarians and dealers in antiquities
and works of art, such as Rosenthal, Merzbacher
and Helbing, to name only the most prominent
among them. In their various special lines they
possessed, in addition to their intensively conducted
business operations, a renown as outstanding
experts and connoisseurs, whose far-reaching influence in cultural matters spread beyond the bound-
aries of Germany. This association of cultural
with business development reveals the condition
of Jewish life, and its widespread presence in the
city of Munich is characteristic of the cultural life
of this capital. One of these leading figures,
Abraham Merzbacher (fl. 1885), was, prior to his
activities as a numismatist, Rabbi in Ansbach.
His library of Jewish literature was of great value,
and upon his death was acquired by the municipal
library of Frankfort. The important scientific
activities of Raphael Nathan Rabbinowicz made
possible his munificent contributions.

A relative of his was Gottfried Merzbacher (1843–
1920) who, starting as an amateur Alpinist, became
an authority as an explorer.

These outstanding and successful men do not
by any means exhaust the Jewish individuals who
were associated with the cultural development of
the city. We have to content ourselves with indicating a few of the foremost or typical representatives.

Together with these must be named several individuals who associated themselves specially with Jewish interests, such as devotion to distinctive Jewish scholarship, or to legal studies for the purpose of bettering the conditions of Jewish existence. Among the most distinguished of the latter was the jurist, Jacob Gotthelf who, in the middle of the 19th century, wrote several important books on Jewish legal and constitutional history in the interest of the efforts made to establish Jewish emancipation. Siegmund Henle (born in Munich, 1821; died there, 1901; ennobled, 1882) was also a valiant champion for the betterment of Jewish conditions. He was a lawyer by profession and was frequently consulted on legal matters by the reigning family. In 1873 he was elected a member of the Bavarian Diet, being allied with the liberal party. He was active by word and pen in furthering the cause of Jewish emancipation. The prominent place attained by him in this rigorously Catholic land gives evidence of the close relationship existing between Catholic and liberal minds in the Munich of that day. It was in this time that Ignaz von Döllinger, Catholic priest and university Professor (1799–1890), delivered his significant academic address on *The Jews in Europe* (1881). As recently as 1846 Döllinger had spoken before the Diet in opposition to Jewish emancipation. The relation of the Munich Jewish Community with the Christian circles dominant in cultural life of the city had changed so quickly. With Döllinger, mention should be made of the famous political economist

Lujo Brentano (born, 1844), who also interpreted in a liberalistic sense the rôle of the Jews in the economic life of Europe, and who, as a member of the university faculty, exerted a strong influence upon large numbers of Jewish students.

Discussions of internal Jewish problems were also conducted during this period of emancipation along generally cultural lines. As early as 1812 it was decided by the congregational leaders that the German language be used in the transaction of their affairs. One of the active congregational leaders of the time, Josef Hirsch Pappenheimer, directed that the prayer book of Dr. Alexander Behr be printed with the title *Tägliche Gebete der Israeliten* (Daily Prayers of the Israelites, 1827). Samuel Hessel's death at about this time had caused a vacancy in the rabbinate. In the new congregational election in 1826, the candidates were Rabbi Hirsch Aub (1796–1876) of Bayersdorf, who was elected to the office, and Hirsch Guggenheimer, the Rabbi of Kriegshaber. During his lengthy incumbency of this pulpit, Aub lived through the entire period of the rise of German Jewry in general, and was active in reorganizing the Jewish congregation in Munich. In the gradual decline of rabbinical scholarship and the rise of secular culture, it became his function to maintain the authority of the rabbinate in the face of the constantly increasing influence of the laity. Repeated suggestions were made in his day that a Rabbinical Seminary be established in Munich. Nothing came of this, however. The existing conditions made it incumbent upon

Aub to devote himself in larger measure to congregational politics than to scholarly problems. More peaceful was the time in which his successor Josef Perles (born, 1835, in Hungary, died, 1894, in Munich) functioned in this pulpit, to which he had been called in 1871. His scholarly sphere of activity embraced the language and antiquities of the Talmud, and his sterling publications received well merited recognition. His wife, Rosalie, who survived him for many years, was the translator of English writings on Jewish subjects.

The pursuit of strictly Jewish scholarship in Munich remained as before in largest measure in the hands of personalities of Eastern extraction. Raphael Nathan Rabbinowicz (1835–1888) was a native of Lithuania. His sphere of activity lay in talmudic studies. The 16 volumes of his *Dikduke Soferim* are devoted to the deviations of the later editions of the Talmud from the uncensored Ms. of 1342, preserved in the National Library of Munich. Of high value is his editorial work on the Responsa of R. Meir of Rothenburg.

Heinrich Ehrentreu (1854–1927) was a native of Hungary, and officiated after 1885 as Rabbi of Munich. He completed the 16th volume of the *Dikduke Soferim* after the death of Rabbinowicz. His lectures on the Talmud were published in 1928 under the title *Minhat Pittim*.

A glance at the intellectual development of the Jews of Munich, Augsburg and Regensburg reveals the following: In the course of the 19th century Munich attained a predominant place, not alone in its relation to the above named Bavarian cities, but as regards all of Southern Germany. This applies not only to intellectual culture generally, but also to Jewish scholarship in particular. The latter, was, however, even in Munich represented by the work of isolated personalities. Neither previously nor at a later date were the conditions in the Jewish population of Munich more favorable for Jewish scholarship than elsewhere. Practically all the active workers in this field came from Eastern Europe. Not until the most recent time do we note, among those of the generation born about 1900, a participation by members of German Jewish circles in Jewish learning, not, however, so much in the domain of talmudic studies as before, but rather along lines of the philosophy of religion, pedagogy and history. The older generations of German-Jewish origin were, on the contrary, strongly attracted, in the course of the 19th century, by general scholarship. The course of affairs might have assumed a different aspect if the suggestion made during the discussions on Jewish emancipation had been realized, that a Jewish Theological Department be established at the University of Munich.

CHAPTER VI

COMMUNAL DEVELOPMENTS

A. REGENSBURG

If we give precedence to Regensburg in the following pages, it is because we are following along the line of historical development. Of our two Bavarian cities, the Jewry of Regensburg experienced its completest flowering at an earlier date than did that of Augsburg. A comprehensive survey of their gradual growth and decline reveals a common development of the Regensburg Jewry with that of the city itself. In the earlier Middle Ages, Regensburg was the residential city of the kings and dukes, and lustrous as a "far-reaching, glistening candelabrum", in the designation given in an old ecclesiastical document. Today it ranks, on the basis of a population of about 80,000 inhabitants, seventh among the cities of Bavaria, and as regards its Jewish population of about 500, as the sixth.

The first actual record of the presence of Jews in Regensburg dates back to the year 981. This is the authorization given by Emperor Otto II for the purchase of a piece of land belonging to the Jew Samuel by the oldest and most famous Regensburg monastery, St. Emeram.[66] It cannot be conclusively proven that this Samuel was actually a resident of Regensburg. Unquestionable evidence of the existence of a Jewish settlement in Regensburg is, however, provided in the record of a gift to the same monastery by a Christian citizen in the year 1020. The presentation of this piece of land is definitely described as "adjacent to the dwelling houses of the Jews".

A clearer insight into the living conditions of the Jews is afforded by a notation in the middle of the 11th century. At about that time a Rabbi Hiyyah traveled from Regensburg to Russia in connection with business transactions. Of him it is reported: "This is the decision given by Rabbi Kalonymos Shabbatai ha-Hazzan in Hungary regarding R. Hiyyah of Regensburg and his brother Jacob. They arrived on Friday with their non-Jewish hirelings, i. e. Christian escorts, and their Jewish associates, and came to a halt on the opposite shore of the Danube because of the breaking of a wheel on one of their wagons. As they entered the city on Friday evening, the congregation was just leaving the House of Prayer. No one extended a greeting to them, and on the following (Sabbath) morning they were not permitted to enter the synagogue. After the Sabbath evening service they came to do penance, and it was decided that they should fast for 50 days and be scourged".[67]

A report by an Emeram monk about the year 1050 tells of a Regensburg Jew named Abraham as having repeatedly reviled Jesus. This probably refers to a religious discussion.

The Jews were also affected by the persecutions that raged at the time of the crusade in 1096; to

how great great an extent is however uncertain.
It is also not definitely ascertainable whether the
permission granted by Emperor Henry in 1097,
"during his stay in Regensburg on his return from
Italy", that Jews who had been forcibly compelled
to accept baptism be allowed to return to the Jewish
fold, had special reference to the Jews of Regensburg.[68] The same uncertainty applies to the protest
made by Pope Clement III against this provision.

Indicative of an established economic status, and
hence a residence of considerable duration, is the
recorded transaction of a loan of 500 silver marks
made in the year 1107 to the Archbishop of Prague
by Jews of Regensburg against a pledge of five
palliums. Also indicating a consolidated Jewish
settlement is the circumstance that a property
owned by the Prül monastery is referred to as
situated *ad Judaeos*,[69] i. e., no doubt, adjacent to
the Jewish city. Reference to established habits
of Jewish trading is contained in a Privilege granted
the Regensburg Jews in 1182 by Emperor Frederick
I, permitting them to trade "in accordance with
established usage, in gold, silver and all sorts of
wares".[70] This Privilege was subsequently renewed
by Frederick II (1216) and King Henry (1230).

The contemporaneous high development of the
city of Regensburg and its influence upon the legal
position of the Jews is revealed in two royal Privileges of that period which were renewed by all
the later kings. In the year 1207 King Philip
allowed the city, along with other Privileges, to
impose taxes upon the clergy and the Jews insofar

as they were engaged in trading activities.[71] In
1251, King Conrad authorized the city to com-
mandeer for military defence the services of clergy-
men and Jews.[72] These are the earliest recorded
decisions touching upon the relation existing between the city and its Jewry.

In the year 1210, the Jews exchanged with the
St. Emeram monastery a plot of ground for use as a
burial place or any other required purpose. For
this site the Jews gave in addition to a sum of
money, with which the monastery redeemed a
mortgaged farmland, a house that was designated
Herberge der Juden (The Jewish Shelter) and which
was surrounded by Jewish dwellings. This house
was, as theretofore, to be rented only to Jews.
Jews from other localities might also be interred
in this burial ground. As witnesses to this convey-
ance, concluded with Abraham and his associates,
there functioned in addition to the twenty-two
designated Jews, "various other Jews and Christians". The assumption that all the Regensburg
Jews had acted as witnesses in this matter appears
therefore to be erroneous. But it is presumable
that the twenty-two Jews designated were Jewish
taxpayers. One may estimate therefore that the
entire number of Jews was about 100.

The acquired plot of ground was located in the
Pauzanswinkel, i. e. in the northwestern section of
the Jewish quarter, but spread some distance south-
ward, as it clearly included the site of the later
synagogue structure. For, when in 1227 the Pope
took under consideration the complaint against the

land-purchase of 1210,—the monastery having
charged that the Jews had secured possession of
this property illegally—it was asserted that the
Jews had constructed a synagogue and cemetery
on this land. In 1225 the Jews acquired from the
Nuns' Convent Obermünster an additional piece of
ground "opposite their *Schul* (Synagogue)". The
tendency toward a consolidation of the community
is revealed by the fact that in this instance there
appear as purchasers "Meister Aaron and the entire
Jewish congregation". One recognizes in this
Meister Aaron the Aharon of Regensburg,[73] who is
referred to in Hebrew literature. Among the witnesses to this transaction there appears also the
name of the Talmudist, Baruk ben Isaac. The
contract carries the names of ten Jews and one
Jewess as witnesses.

The cemetery, the ground for which had been
acquired in 1210, lay therefore immediately adjacent
to the Jewish quarter of the city. An apparently
reliable record reveals the existence at an earlier
period of two other Jewish burial grounds, the one
on the farther side of the rivulet Regen, which had
given the city its name, and the other toward the
south on the highway to Abach.[74]

According to the 13th century records covering
its third decade, an unfavorable turn appears to
have developed in the status of the Jews. The
Privilege accorded them in 1182 had assured to
them, in addition to trading rights in precious
metals, the right to trade in "all sorts of commercial materials". The confirmation of Jewish

rights in the year 1230 mentions only the trading
in precious metals, but says nothing regarding other
articles of commerce. Might this have been a
chance omission on the part of the official recorder?
Hardly. In the first half of the century the church
enforced its decree prohibiting the payment of
interest; in 1254 the commercial cities of the Rhineland regulated Jewish money-lending. In this period
the Jews of Regensburg must also have changed
from mercantile trading to money-lending. We
must therefore conclude that the omission in the
Privilege recorded in 1230 proves that the Jews
regarded as valueless the inclusive trading rights
previously vouchsafed them. The privilege of
trading in precious metals does not affect this conclusion, as this was bound up with matters of
coinage and banking, and these in turn with the
possession of cash. It was a period in which the
Jews still played an important rôle in matters of
governmental coinage. At the same time there is
no indication that the Privilege of 1230 implied an
intentional restriction in the commercial activities
of the Jews, as its provisions are on the whole favorable to them. It directs distinctly that they be
called for trial only before magistrates elected by
themselves; that Christians, in charges brought
against Jews, be required to include a Jewish
witness; and that Jews should be regarded as the
owners of real estate that had been in their undisputed possession for ten years. It is to be taken for

granted that this last provision points to the impugning in 1227 of the land purchase of 1210.

At that time there were manifested in Regensburg, as in other localities, the effects of internal dissension which for many centuries, since the reign of Frederick II, weakened the strength of the German Empire. In the dangers that continually menaced the Empire, from the time of its great conflict with Pope Gregory IX, questions relating to Jewish revenues together with those regarding jurisdiction over the Jews served repeatedly as grounds for political conflicts and reconciliations. One of the earlier instances of such political tactics was the hypothecation of the revenues of the Regensburg Jewry by King Henry in 1233 to Bishop Siegfried of Regensburg.[75] This was associated with the then inimical political attitude of the Emperor toward Bavaria and the municipalities. For almost a century thereafter a conflict continued between the bishops of Regensburg and the dukes of Bavaria on the subject of control of the Regensburg Jewry.

Alongside of these three authorities invested with power over the Jews (Emperor, Duke, Bishop), there appeared as the youngest of the political powers of the period, the city. It was preparing to battle with the Bishop and the Duke for the establishment of its own independence, and eventually secured, in consequence of a political realignment of the contending factions, the support of the King.

Since that time all the forces were in evidence
which, in the sequel, through either compromise
or conflict, determined the destinies of the Regensburg Jewry: Empire, Territory, Church and the
Municipal administration.

A conflict between the dukes and the bishops
regarding Jewish control, which was probably
precipitated by · dissensions regarding coinage,—
details are not known—reached a provisional conclusion in 1265 through a compromise arrived at
between Duke Henry and Bishop Leo. The former
relinquished a claim of 700 lbs. for the loss of
Jewish revenues which he had suffered through
Leo's predecessor, receiving in exchange an equiv-
alent indemnity.[76] The episcopal control of the Jews
was thereafter practically extinguished. There
continued only an episcopal right to the payment
of an annual 30 lbs. out of the Jewish tax revenues.
The evidence dates from a later time, but the claim
goes back to rights of a much earlier period.[77] In
the year 1297 a war broke out between the city
and the Duke, precipitated by a tax assessment
levied by the latter against the Jews, which was
ended by arbitration on October 19, 1297. The
city was subsequently reimbursed by the Duke for
damages sustained during the war, the latter
receiving from the city, on his part, an indemnity
of 1000 lbs. for damages suffered, and from the
Jews a payment of 2000 lbs. The latter payment
was subject to the condition that the Duke be
required to assist in the defense of both the city
and its Jewry, in the event of the King's refusal to

approve this payment and a demand for payment
to himself of another 2000 lbs. The starting point
of this quarrel was the assertion by the Duke that
the King, in recognition of the former's services in
the war against France, had accorded him a grant
to demand of the Jews the sum specified.[78]

It is clear from this incident that at that time
the King exercised an undisputed right to levy
taxes against the Jews of Regensburg, in any event
insofar as such levies were occasioned by extraordinary revenue requirements. There must, however, have existed even then an older Bavarian
right of taxation, upon which the above mentioned
arbitrament of 1265 may be founded.[79]

Ecclesiastical influences upon the fate of the Jews
continued upon another basis despite the relinquish-
ing of Jewish sovereignty on the part of the Bishop.
The resolutions adopted at the Vienna Church
Council in 1267 applied, among others, to the
ecclesiastical province of Salzburg which included
the bishopric of Regensburg.[80]

The agreement of 1297 indicates that, following
the Interregnum (1256–73), the King assumed his
rights over the Jews of Regensburg with intensified
energy. Already in the year following his accession,
King Rudolf confirmed to them their former
franchises, and that too in the previous form, which
included not only their right to trade in precious
metals but permitted them to trade in all other
kinds of goods. A copy of this Privilege formerly
in Jewish hands, is still in existence. It contains
the Hebrew notation, *Ketab ha-melek al ha-sehorah*

(The King's writing concerning trade). This would indicate that the provisions affecting their civic legal rights, also contained in the document, were not as important to the Jews as was the section covering their trading privileges. Are we to see in the new privilege to trade in goods a temporary reversion in the economic specialization of the Jew, or is it merely an accident of diplomatic expression?

It is, however, possible that even the Jewish notation may not afford conclusive evidence regarding the economic condition of the Jews, but that it bears witness only to the commercial character of the Privilege in contradistinction to another royal Privilege of 1275. Referring to the well-known bulls of Innocent IV and Gregory X, this Privilege declared that the Jews shed no Christian blood, and that no Jew be punished upon such a charge unless the prosecution included Jewish witnesses. In a procedural sense this was merely confirmatory of older regulations relating specifically to ritual-murder charges. The records of Regensburg contain no reference to any charge of this nature having been brought against Jews of that city. If this be not due to a lacuna in the records, one is compelled to think that these provisions were adopted as preventive measures in view of similar charges increasingly brought against Jews in Germany during that period.

It was during the reign of Rudolf of Habsburg that the ritual-blood superstition raged throughout the land, making its appearance now here now there

and resulting in bloodshed at some place or other
almost every year. In the year 1275, at the time
the above mentioned Privilege was issued, the
blood-accusation reared its head in Lorch, which
was located below Passau and at no great distance
from Regensburg. The latter was the nearest-lying
city containing a large Jewish community. It may
be readily assumed that the happenings in Lorch
were connected with the Privilege. In the neighboring city of Munich a similar accusation a decade
later (1285) led to the downfall of the Jews.

For Germany this period marked the beginning
of a progressive dissolution. Many royal rights
and titular powers had to be hypothecated to defray
the costs of maintaining the Imperial policy. The
most available recourse for such purposes was the
right of levying taxes upon the Jews, associated
with the legal fees of Jews and Jewish control in
general. The Regensburg Jewish control was, in
the year 1323, for these reasons, diverted to the
Bavarian crown. It must, however, be borne in
mind that this regulation could have been influenced
by the above mentioned older Bavarian rights.
The episcopal pretensions to control of Jewish
affairs were entirely extinguished in those days,
although there remained in force an annual taxing
privilege to the amount of 30 lbs.

The Jewish community was not constitutionally
incorporated with the municipality, although in an
economic sense this was the case. As late as 1229 a
house and building site was leased by S. Johannes of
Regensburg to the Jew Abraham, *"iure Judaeorum"*

only.[81] On the other hand, in 1288, a loan was given
by the Jew Gnenlin to the Rohr monastery *secundum
consuetudinem Ratisponae et totius provinciae* (according to the custom of Ratisbon and the whole
province). The Augsburg city administration had
regulated the economic relations between Jews and
Christians in accordance with its legal enactments
of 1276. In Regensburg, owing to the more difficult
political conditions of the Jews, such regulations
were not adopted, but the growing supremacy of
the municipal influence is also discernible here.

The civic influence was not yet a decisive one,
as is shown by the fact that Jews were privileged
to affix their own seals to documents, a right that
was not rescinded until a later period. Until almost
1400, seals (in principle, therefore, the legal right)
were possessed not only by individual Jews, but
also by the Jewish communities of Regensburg and
Augsburg. The last Jewish seal of Regensburg is
of the year 1397. Seals affixed with wax served in
place of signatures, but required as a protection
against fraud the attestation of Jews and non-Jews.
We are thus made acquainted with the names of
many Regensburg Jews which would otherwise be
unknown to us. The Regensburg Jewish seals[82]—
not many in number—that are still in existence,
contain the following emblems: Half Moon, Star,
Flower and Cock. The seal of the Regensburg
Jewish community was circular in form, and in
addition to the legend inscribed about its edge was
stamped in the center with Star and Half Moon.
It is not likely that these emblems were of independ-

1. The Community Seal of Regensburg.

2. Old Sketch of the Mediaeval Synagogue in Regensburg.

ent Jewish origin. The designs were probably the
work of earlier Christian seal engravers. The origin
of the Half Moon in the Jewish seal may be traced
to the Turkish military emblem, which in turn is
based upon a text of the Koran. This conclusion
may be strengthened by the fact that these Jewish
seals are found only in the time of the later crusades,
and that the increasingly prevalent fashion of
heraldic insignia in general was greatly influenced
by oriental designs.

Recorded Jewish business pursuits in Regensburg
at the end of the 13th century were along banking
lines of extended scope. In 1288 the Rohr monastery
executed a bond guaranteeing the sum of 100 lbs.
to the Jew Gnenlin and his sons Jacob and Maenes-
sin for Counts Hals and Abensberg.[83] In 1291 a
payment of 52 lbs. is made by Duke Louis to the
Jew Efferlein in redemption of a pledge. In 1297
the Archbishop of Salzburg received 200 lbs. from
the Jew Samson of Mühldorf and a Christian of
that city. The money was delivered to the Regensburg Jews Atschim (Hayyim) and Jacob, to whom
it was owing by Count Ulrich von Abensberg as
surety for Duke Otto. In 1302 the Regensburg
Jews, Jacob, Gaedel and Fraeudel, executed a
release in the amount of 50 lbs. for which the
Archbishop of Salzburg had become indebted to
them and Atschim for Conrad von Ernfels. In
1306 the sum of 50 lbs. is paid by the Archbishop
to the Jew Gärlm (of Regensburg?) for the redemption of a sawmill in Sulzbach belonging to the
nobleman von Lichtenberg. In 1313 the imperial

vicar, King John of Bohemia, granted permission
to the Bishop of Regensburg to redeem a cross that
had been pawned, together with other regalia, with
Nicolaus de Turri, a citizen of Prague, and rehypoth-
ecated by the latter with Regensburg Jews, to the
"ignominy of the Lord", a genuine section of whose
cross was asserted to have formed a part of the
pledged article.[84] In 1317 the Obermünster Convent
in Regensburg sold its right to collect the dues for
the purpose of canceling its Jewish indebtedness.
In the subsequent years there are authentic records
of Jewish loans as follows: in 1321 four patricians
of Regensburg borrowed on behalf of the Hanse,
i. e., the Chamber of Commerce, 15 lbs. from the
Jew Seibot of Prague, in Regensburg, and his
daughter Leah, at the customary interest rate
of 43 ⅓%, to be used for an embassy to the King
of Bohemia. In the same year and also on behalf
of the Hanse, another citizen borrowed 11 lbs.
51 pf. from the Jew Izzerlein, Aaron's son, and
his brothers. This loan was repaid about 1 ½
years later.[85] In 1322 there followed a similar
loan by Slümlein, a son-in-law of Aaron. On the
repayment on February 14, 1323, of this loan,
which had been made on January 13, 1322, interest
amounting to 1 lb. was added, which represented
exactly 27 ³/₂₀%, not however, the 43 ⅓%
agreed upon, which would have been the Jewish
maximum rate of interest, viz., 2 pf. weekly per lb.
In 1324 Conrad of Schwarzenberg borrowed 16
lbs. from the Jew Musch (=Moses), to be repaid
at the end of three months at a delayed payment

interest rate of 86 ⅔% (a weekly rate of 4 pf. per
lb.). In 1424 the son of the Burgomaster borrowed
23 lbs. from the Jew Wölflein for the purpose of
liquidating other obligations. He returned the
money slightly after a month's time with an added
interest payment of 6 ½%, essentially more than
the 43 ⅓% yearly interest exacted by the terms
of the loan, in which the customary weekly rate
of interest is definitely stated. The content of the
bond of indebtedness reveals the fact that the son
of the Burgomaster was in serious financial straits,
and it appears that there was in the modern phras-
eology, an exaction of usury by the creditor, which,
however, was tolerable for the debtor in view of
the limited term of the loan. In the before-mentioned Schwarzenberger case there was also, it is
true, an exorbitant interest charge, but that was in
the nature of a penalty imposed for delay in the
repayment of the loan, in accordance with the
then current practice. This was, therefore, not a
case of usury in the modern sense of the term.
The 27% interest charge made by the Jew Slümlein
in 1323 was entirely proper. Further investigations
along these lines, the results of which will be given
in another place, furnish additional evidence of
occasional cases of usury alongside of legitimate
banking business, but they were not prevalent.

That credits granted by the Jews could not be
given at a low rate of interest is made manifest by
the fact that the conditions surrounding such loans
were frequently of a most complicated nature.
A characteristic instance may be mentioned here.

Two old Bavarian nobles of the houses of Fraun-
berger and Preising, whose names are often found
in the Jewish annals of Regensburg, were indebted
to the Christian firm of Dietrich Steinkircher. This
debt had been guaranteed by the episcopal foundation of Freising. The debtors subsequently borrowed 900 lbs. from the Regensburg Jew Nahman
and his associates, subject to a 17 ½% annual
amortization, and gave as security the income due
them from the estates of the bishopric of Freising.
The Duke pledged himself to protect the Jewish
interests in the event of any one interfering with
the income from the estates of the bishopric. By
the year 1338 the amount of the indebtedness had
grown to 1146 fl., presumably owing to failure to
make the annual payments. The Jews were empowered to appoint an administrator, for the
taking over of the rentals. At a later period no such
far-reaching rights, which ran counter to the decisions of the Church Councils, at any rate to their
spirit, are to be found. The details of these business
involvements are not entirely clear. It would
appear that the Steinkircher firm, in default of the
repayment of the loan, borrowed the capital from
the Jews at the risk of the debtor and transferred
its securities to the Jewish creditors.

Another business venture undertaken by a Jewish banking syndicate was the financial rehabilitation of the Regensburg bishopric in 1377. During
the Bishop's incumbency the foundation had developed a deficit and the dean and chapter of the
Cathedral were in consequence compelled to take

over the usufruct of its properties and the indemni-
fication of its creditors. Among the latter, besides
several Christians, the names are given of the Jews
Gnendlein and Jöslein, to whom we shall have
repeated occasion to refer, and the Jew David
Steuss of Vienna, called the favorite of the Viennese
ducal court. Unfortunately there is no detailed
information available regarding the nature and
scope of this rehabilitation. It may, however, be
taken for granted that in this instance also the
claims of the creditors were satisfied out of the
income derived from the episcopal properties. It is
certain that in many cases the larger Jewish credit
establishments of the period adopted forms of
incorporation or partnership. An instance of what
may be called international financial combination is
found in the above-mentioned association with
David Steuss. It was often in the form of a family
organization that activities were conducted in the
realms of high finance, such as the families of
Nahman of Munich, residing since 1338 in Regensburg; the Efferlein, Aaron, Mändlein families, and
others. During the period from about 1300 to
1360, the debtors of such associations were the city
of Regensburg itself, the bishopric of Regensburg,
the archbishopric of Salzburg and the Bavarian
ducal house. The names of Regensburg Christian
citizens also appear as associates in the larger
Jewish credit engagements. Disputes between
creditors and debtors were also not lacking. Repressive measures adopted by the city against Mändlein
of Salzburg (1334) are clearly associated with

credits advanced by him. The temporary enmity manifested in 1346 by the Archbishop of Salzburg against the Regensburg Jewry is probably traceable to similar circumstances. Rarely do the records reveal with any clearness the detailed arrangements of such credit transactions. Even the stipulated and the actually paid interest charges, which were not in any sense always identical, are not as a rule ascertainable. It is to be assumed that especially in the case of higher governing functionaries there was the same irresponsibility or carelessness regarding repayments of loans as there was in their creation. In a loan made to the city about 1340 by the Jew Efferlein, an annual interest charge of 30% was agreed upon. A loan received by Heinrich Portner of Augsburg in 1345,[86] in which the Regensburg citizen Rüdiger Reich (who was himself in temporary charge, as pledge holder, of a portion of the Jewish taxes) was in some way interested, bore a yearly interest charge of 25%. At this point we must rest satisfied with the illustrations here recorded revealing the regular and far-reaching scope of the Jewish banking business in its relations with ruling princes, ecclesiastical corporations, nobles, municipalities and city patricians.

That efforts were made to maintain orderly relations with the Regensburg Jews is indicated by the effective protection accorded them by the city authorities in all the emergencies of the time. When in 1298 the Rindfleisch hordes marched on the city with the avowed intention of exterminating the Jews, and asserted that they were obeying the will of God, the city authorities demanded that they furnish unequivocal signs to this effect. In like manner, when in the period of the 1336–38 persecutions, the neighboring Jewish communities of Deggendorf and Straubing fell victims to these attacks, the Regensburg Jews remained unscathed. They were also protected when, in 1342, during the Auerian disturbances in Regensburg, an uprising of the populace against both the patriciate and the Jews was threatened. In the period of greatest danger, at the time of the Black Death persecutions of the Jews, 237 of the leading citizens of Regensburg united for their protection. This body, which must have included almost the entire group of Regensburg's foremost social section, as the total population of the city barely approximated 6000, guaranteed, in an impressive manifesto, protection to the Jews of Regensburg (October 3, 1349). While an attempt had also been made in Regensburg to bring to trial a ritual-murder charge, this was suppressed by the court. On October 25, 1348, the city authorities took such action "as was right" against a man who asserted that he had offered to sell a boy to the Jews.[87]

The Regensburg sources do not afford the slightest evidence that the crisis of 1348–49 might be referred to as a pronounced "credit crisis of most barbarous character". It was to the incitement of the common people, or poorer classes, that the Jews in many places fell victims, and it was just this lower class in the Regensburg of that time—as it was in Augsburg—which is not found among the debtors of the Jews. But even the peasantry in the environs of the city, which was frequently active in the Jewish persecutions, does not appear to have figured to any extent as debtors of the Jews until a later time. The blame attaching to the reigning princes for neglecting the legal protection of the Jews has been referred to in the foregoing. The city of Regensburg also secured itself in 1349—as it had in 1342 during the so-called Auerian disturbances— against liability to the Bavarian rulers in case they were unable to provide protection to the Jews against a populace excited by the pestilence and its associated manifestations.

By the protection accorded its Jews by the city of Regensburg at that time, it maintained the peace both against the calamities threatened by a demoralized populace and aggressions on the part of the princely rulers. For in the same manner as many other rulers, the Bavarian dukes were in the habit of holding the cities liable if they thought their financial interests were endangered by happenings in the Jewish quarters.[88] There still existed at that time in the memory of the municipal authorities the claim that had been made in 1339 by the Duke to the possessions of the despoiled Straubing Jewish victims which had allegedly been transferred to Regensburg; and there had lacked but little for the precipitation of an armed conflict such as had been provoked in 1297. The danger was the more imminent inasmuch as since that time the Jews of Regensburg, following the hypothecations made by Emperor Louis the Bavarian (1323 to about

1329), had become subjects of the Bavarian dukes. They paid the dukes an annual interest of 200 lbs., and were compelled to relinquish their right of electing the so-called Jewish judges. This Jewish court also represented an income for the dukes in dues and penalties.

Through this hypothecation to the dukes, the former episcopal Jewish control which had still in 1265, as we have seen, been a subject of contention, was definitely abrogated. The year 1320 provides the last recorded episcopal pronouncement bearing reference to a clerical subordination of the Jews. Somewhat woefully the Bishop is constrained shortly thereafter (1327) to forgo passing a direct sentence upon Jews accused of assaulting a cleric, and instead has to content himself with forbidding the Christian, as *homo religiosus*, to have any further association with the guilty ones.[89]

The protection accorded the Jews in the frequent dangers to which they were subjected, together with the weakened authority of the Bavarian ducal house following the death of Louis the Bavarian and the rapid growth of an economically developed citizenry after the depopulation caused by the Black Death, resulted in an increasing importance of the city as contrasted with the diminishing influence of the ducal house. It was the city that during the next few decades exercised the authoritative rôle in matters connected with Jewish control, not so much as a consequence of its legal rights as of the increased political power it had acquired. A distinct policy in matters affecting the settle-

ment of Jews is discernible in the municipal pronouncements between the years 1356 and 1380,
especially noticeable when the city had great need
for credit. The municipality had in 1345 taken over
portions of the ducal and episcopal Jewish revenues.
Since 1377, it had on its part given an annual
guarantee of protection to the Jews. The relative
powers exercised over the Jews by the Emperor,
the dukes and the city were by no means clearly
defined. They were regulated by customary law,
and the most powerful and most active among the
competing powers at the time usually controlled
the situation.

It was in matters of taxation that the new course
of affairs was most clearly indicated. The older
levies, such as payments in kind and personal labor
requirements on the part of the Jews, the contributions of pepper and wearing apparel, appear to
have been discontinued and to have been replaced
by money payments. In the reconstructed administrative personnel there disappears the Jewish
constable (*Judenscherge*), i. e., doubtless, the Christian functionary who in legal disputes between Jews
and Christians acted as sheriff and server of judicial
summonses. This function was transferred to the
sheriffs of the municipal courts. It appears that
about the year 1380, they were considering a new
form of Jewish oath in Regensburg.[90]

A particular policy adopted by the city in relation
to Jewish settlements is revealed in the records of
the 3rd, 5th, 7th and 8th decades of the 14th century. In these times the public, and occasionally,

the private demand for money was especially urgent,
the former in consequence of the civil wars waged
in the reign of King Louis, and later on account of
the conflicts growing out of the confederation of the
cities, in which conflicts Regensburg was actively
involved. The private demand for capital is ascribed
to the destruction of numerous economic advantages
owing to the pestilence of 1348–49.

In the year 1338, the city ordered the Jew Nahman
of Munich to take up his residence in Regensburg.
This is supposed to have been in compliance with
a suggestion made by the Jews who did not wish
to dispense with the revenues paid by Nahman,
who also had commercial interests in Regensburg.[91]
At this time the city borrowed substantial sums
from the Jews Efferlein, Michel of Straubing,
Nahman of Munich, Musch Payer of Vienna and
others, in the raising of which funds a large group
of Jewish capitalists were compelled to unite, the
exaction of this loan bearing all the earmarks of
a compulsory assessment. In the year 1356 the
city commissioned the Jewess Chändlein and her
associates to effect an arrangement with incoming
Jews, i. e. to determine in the name of the city the
amount of the tax they should pay in consideration
of their being permitted to locate there.[92] In this
instance one should not necessarily conclude that
the city desired to secure for itself and its citizens
new sources of financial revenue or credit, but its
purpose was rather the liquidating of tax arrearages.
For in consequence of the complete disorganization
of their economic existence by reason of the pesti-

lence and the prevailing unrest, the Jews had become
impoverished and the payment of taxes by them
discontinued. It is only on this basis we can explain
that tax arrearages had accumulated with the
annual taxes and had to be later amortized together
with the yearly tax payments. Thus in 1358, the
Regensburg Jew, Aron of Prague, was compelled
to pay yearly taxes and amortization of 13 lbs. and
5 lbs. respectively; Abraham of Räx, 4 lbs. for each;
and Chändlein, 50 lbs. and 5 lbs. respectively.[93]
The large arrearages are due to the fact that these
were owing by wealthy Jews subject to correspond-
ingly larger tax obligations. This situation gave
rise to acrimonious tax disputes among the Jews.
The resident Jews and the city had an equal interest
in attracting to the community as many substantial
tax-paying individuals as they could. The pressure
that had been brought to bear upon Nahman of
Munich has already been mentioned. A different
experience was that of Smärl of Vienna. He was
threatened with a tax levy in Regensburg, but
secured the intervention of Duke Albrecht of
Austria, who addressed a letter to the city of
Regensburg in his behalf. The issue of this case is
not known. The lack of permanent domicile for
the Jews in those days made possible the city's
policy of inviting them to become residents.
Nahman attached the appellation "of Munich"
to his name. His son, Efferlein, made his home
temporarily with his father-in-law, Aron, in Salzburg, and the authorities of Regensburg sent him
a letter of indebtedness in 1339 to that city. Aron's

other son-in-law, Mändlein, resided in Regensburg,
where he purchased, in 1345, houses from the
Jewish community.[94] The Jew Feyfel (i. e. Vivus
or Hayyim), whose financial operations about the
year 1360 were the most extensive of any in Regensburg, and whose widow and sons continued the
business for a number of years following his death,
was known as Feyfel "of Nuremberg".[95] Moses
of Egg and the before-mentioned Aron of Prague,
and Abraham of Räx, also give evidence of the
instability of Jewish domicile. In contrast with
these, however, Regensburg Jews are also found
to have made their homes in other cities, thus
Jacob of Regensburg lived in Landshut, about the
year 1370. This fluctuation of Jewish domicile was
not directly provoked by the happenings of 1349,
but was intensified by them.

These changes of residence on the part of the
Jews proved advantageous to both the city and
the rulers. A customs ordinance of about 1365[96]
provides that all the Jews of Northern and Southern Bavaria who were engaged in trade in Regensburg be required to pay an *ad valorem* tax of 1 ⅔%,
such tax not to be imposed upon Jews resident in
Regensburg. There is distinct reference made in
this document to the books owned by the Jews.
The inference here is clear that a tax on household
furnishings, at least, is also imposed by the terms
of the enactment, there being no indication of the
levying of this tax upon generally established Jewish business. It is at the same time not improbable
that, associated with the economic tendency of the

period, there was a weakening of the control exercised by the guilds and a consequent opportunity created temporarily for an extension of Jewish business ventures. It should be borne in mind that it was just at this time that Duke Rudolf IV enforced restrictions upon the guilds in the neighboring Austrian territory,[97] and that in the same period the city of Regensburg interrupted its policy of attracting Jews to its precincts. The latter circumstance might point to an economic recovery, a decreasing need of money, and the consequent decline of interest in the admission of Jews between about 1360 and 1375, unless the incident recorded is merely a fortuitous reference of the chronicler. There are no records during this period of a civic policy relating to the settlement of Jews in Regensburg. After the year 1376 the city returned again to this policy. Here, as in the customs ordinance of about 1365, there is again manifested an opposition to the ducal interests. In 1376 the entire City Council met with the Prior of the Augustinian Monastery to determine definitely the matter of giving domicile to the Jews Gnendlein and Jössl.[98] The outcome was that the Duke had to accept 350 fl. and grant permission to the two Jews to reside in Regensburg. This sum had to be paid again by the Jews contrary to the agreement originally entered into with the city. The Duke was also required by direction of the Emperor to rescind his claim upon the property of the Jews that had been attached by him. At the same time the Jews of Regensburg received a royal confirma-

tion of the Privileges formerly enjoyed by them,
for which they made a payment of 750 fl. Difficulties
of a similar nature were experienced with the Count
Palatine Rupprecht in 1386, in the matter of the
Jew Noce (Nathan?). Apparently the wealth of
the Jews and their earning power reached such
large proportions that their coming and going had
an important significance.

In this period the following were accorded Jewish
citizenship in Regensburg: Jössel von der Weiden
(1379), the little Pendit (=Baruk) of Augsburg
(1380), Eisack and Vischl of Freising, Mair Hezz
of Würzburg (1381), Mändl of Straubing (1384),
Isserl, Unterkaüfel of Vienna (1385), Gütl, Jewess
of Stein (1385), Jax of Amberg, Güt of Bamberg
and his son Chopfel (Jacob), Noce of Amberg, the
Symonin of Amberg (all 1386), "Meister" Jacob,
Sara of Mülhausen, Heinlein of Weissenburg (1387),
Smärl of Straubing (1390).[99] The cancellations of
Jewish debts ordered by Wenceslaus, and the consequent anxieties and difficulties, are probably
associated with the incoming of Jews after 1384.
The Jews evidently looked to the city of Regensburg for effective protection. There was an undis-
guised *quid pro quo* policy adopted by the authorities.
The city accorded a protection which was sought
by the Jews, but this could be secured to them only
so long as they maintained their financial responsibility. An admonitory complaint recorded by the
secretary of the Regensburg Council about 1380
throws light upon the situation in the following
words: "Consider the Jews, who by day and night

are engaged in working for their own advantage, and yet the city does not put an end to these activities while there is still time". The city, however, was safeguarding its own interests, as it restricted the admission of Jews to a definite period of two to three years. It is obvious that so brief a period for the right of domicile for a people forced to acquire wealth rapidly included dangers for the communal as well as the individual welfare. At the same time the records reveal that the families Nahman-Efferlein, Feyfel and others were during a period of decades subjected to only temporary interruptions of domicile. They must have proven themselves useful members of the community in the lines of their activity.

The extraordinary risks involved in the business of money-lending in those unsettled times of warfare, and the peculiar manner in which the ruling princes were involved in these matters, is revealed in the business records of Jacob of Ulm, who is perhaps identical with the Meister Jacob who came to Regensburg in 1387.[100] By means of a 50% participation in the amount of the loan he managed to bring about the declaration of war by the Duke against his debtor.

One of the most important financial operations of that time was involved in the rehabilitation of the insolvent Regensburg bishopric in the year 1373.[101] The Bishop conveyed to the dean and chapter of the Cathedral, "without the aid and advice of whom he was unable to adjust his affairs," the usufruct of his properties, in consideration of

which the chapter took over the obligation of
satisfying the claims of the creditors Gnendlein,
Jössl, and David Steuss of Vienna, as well as those
of Christian creditors. He also, it appears, arranged
for a loan of 4000 fl. which was taken up by the
city of Regensburg about 1360, at an 8% annual
rate of interest, the city receiving in this transaction
an option on an additional loan of 5000 fl.[102]

After the middle of the century the influence and
position of the Jews were substantially strengthened.
In 1355, on the advice of his vicar, the Regensburg
citizen Stephan Haller in his will directed his heirs
to repay to the Jews 40 lbs. which he had received
from them during a period of four years, and this
"as an act of mercy". In 1352 and 1353 the Jews
had been unable to make payment of their taxes.[103]
In 1358 Friedrich Mautner, who held in pledge
from the dukes the greater part of the Jewish taxes,
remitted the payment of these "for many years"
unpaid tax obligations. The city at the same time
made a similar declaration, explaining in this connection that the impoverishment of the Jews had
been occasioned by the excessive taxes levied against
them by the princes and rulers.

The records of that period give no indication
either that the Jews, as has been frequently assumed,
acted as bankers for the poorer classes. This seems
improbable, as the resources of the Jews, whose
number was limited, were absorbed by large loans
of a public character. In a contemporary balance
sheet of the municipality only 25 taxpayers are
listed, in addition to the above-mentioned new

arrivals in the Jewish community. The acts of
violence to which the Jews were frequently subjected in that troubled time were precipitated in
large measure by the nobles and not by despairing
middle-class citizens. It is not known by whom
the Jewess Chändlein, who had been commissioned
to look after the Jewish revenues in 1356, was
assassinated. In 1371 a Jewish boy was abducted
by a neighboring nobleman in order to extort
money from the child's father to whom he was indebted. The city authorities, however, compelled
the abductor to return the boy. A Christian butcher
who had assaulted a Jew was expelled from the
city. In the year 1439, it was the captain of the
town militia himself who, in the course of a financial
settlement, placed his Jewish creditors under arrest,
put them into a chest together with the body of
one of them who had met his death in the fight,
and carried them off. The city sentenced him to
banishment. He escaped this punishment, however,
through the intercession of the Duke, and only his
servants were executed. It may be that the above-
mentioned acts of violence perpetrated by private
debtors against the Jews provide a possible explanation of the origin of the riches acquired by them.
The amount of interest received on public loans
can hardly account for the accumulation of their
wealth. The interest rate of 8% paid by the Regensburg bishopric for its rehabilitation was moderate
enough according to the usage in those days. In

1381 the city of Regensburg[104]* borrowed 900 fl. from two Jews of Nuremberg at a rate of 17 ⅔%, i. e. a rate about as high as that of the annuities which were guaranteed by the entire resources of the city. If it be not taken for granted that the Jews had accumulated riches through their commercial activities, which the sources of our information do not indicate, then the basis of their increasing affluence in that time must be traced to those private financial transactions with the nobles and members of knightly orders.

The fact that the city of Regensburg, as was the case with other cities, was enabled through money secured from the Jews to prevail in its battles for political dominance, turned the attention of the King to the importance of Jewish capital. To the degree in which the municipality was concerned in maintaining a continually renewable source of credits and taxes by means of the protection of its Jewish inhabitants, it was to the interest of the King to weaken the municipality by the withdrawal of this source of revenue, and at the same time strengthen the royal exchequer. The two so-called Jewish debt cancellations of King Wenceslaus (1387–1400) had their predecessors. An attempted tax levy upon the Jews of Regensburg by Charles IV, in 1373, led to Jewish efforts at evacuation of

* The city was in continual financial difficulties, having had in 1381, against an income of 3277 lbs., disbursements amounting to 4766 lbs.

the city. The city was thus in danger not only of
losing its Jews, but of interference in its affairs on
the part of alien powers, should the Jews be compelled to seek princely protectors. The entire
Jewish community, represented by the before-
mentioned Abraham of Räx, Gnendel, Veivel,
Musch and others, pledged themselves to remain
in the city for a period of twelve more years, and
to depend upon the protection of the city only and
not to lay claim to the protection of the prince.[105]
In this manner the city revoked temporarily, when
it appeared advantageous to its interests, the
provisions of limited domicile. Duke Frederick of
Bavaria had, as holder of the pledges of the Regensburg Jewry, guaranteed his coöperation to the King.
The Jews finally paid the sum of 4000 fl. to the
Emperor. The order of attachment which had
been hanging over them during their refusal to
make payments was rescinded.

In 1381, King Wenceslaus again imposed a tax
levy upon the Jews, and Duke Frederick was once
more deputed to act as his delegate. Against this
measure a protest was again entered by the city.
It was finally agreed to submit the matter to arbitration by the royal tribunal. This resulted in an
agreement between the parties, enjoining upon the
King the definite confirmation of Jewish release
in the matter of state taxation and imposing upon
the city a payment of 4000 fl. chargeable to the
Jews. In consequence of this agreement, the King,

on February 21, 1382, again absolved the Jews
from payment of state taxes, which remained
pledged as before to the Bavarian house.

The large sums of money required for carrying
on the war between the cities, during the decade
covered by the years 1379–1389, resulted in favors
bestowed upon the Jews by the municipal administration. The distress brought about by the war
mobilized the anger of the populace against the
municipal administration as well as against the
Jews. In Swabia 1400 villages had been laid in
ashes during the conflict, and throughout this
region the farmers, upon whose produce the city
was dependent and who had been spared during
the fighting, were driven out by the avaricious
nobles. In the neighboring Nördlingen the magistrate gave free rein to the popular wrath against
the Jews (1384), and for this reason the city was
expelled from the "Swabian Municipal Confederation". In Regensburg, however, the Jews were
again accorded protection.

These circumstances favored a new attempt on
the part of King Wenceslaus. He made fresh
demands upon the Jews, protests against which
were raised by the city, which had made certain
of the support of Duke Albrecht as pledge holder
of the Jewish control. The Duke eventually came
to an agreement with the King, details of which
are lacking, and received from the city in the name
of the Jews the sum of 5800 fl.[106] The city, however,

adopted the precaution of securing assurances from the Duke that he, as pledge holder, would not hold it responsible for its friendly attitude to the King. In addition to all these dissensions, the city had, in May and June of 1384, compelled its wealthiest Jews, namely, Gnendel, Sadia, Meier Hesse and Veivel, to bind themselves by oath not to remove from the city and to deposit with the authorities for safekeeping their jewels and other articles of value, the city reserving the right to dispose of these in accordance "with its wishes". Shortly thereafter the above-named Jews were nevertheless placed under arrest, but were released upon renunciation of their rights in the properties they had turned over to the city. The property thus secured was used by the city to liquidate the annual pensions (*leibgedinge*), approximating 3000 fl.[107] The list of paid up obligations (*ablösungsverzeichnis*) is, however, incomplete. In addition hereto there are to be included the 5800 fl. paid to the Duke. The property loss suffered by the Jews was therefore considerable.

The exactions made by the King in the year 1389 went much further. In May of that year he sent two commissioners to Regensburg as authorized caretakers of the Jews of that city. This action on his part was keenly resented by both the municipality and the Duke, and the latter offered his support to the city in the matter. The King was compelled to content himself with a payment of 4000 fl., in addition to which bonds of indebtedness held by Duke Frederick, the Counts Abensberg and the city of Landshut, standing in the name of

Gnendel and amounting to 7100 fl., were turned
over to the city.[108] Sadia, Gnendl and David signed
as representatives of the Jewish community. The
records are not clear as to the manner in which
this sum was divided between the city, the Duke
and the King. Even so, the King was satisfied
with this arrangement for the period of only a
twelve-month. In the spring and summer of 1390
the King repeatedly haled the municipal authorities
and the Jews before the Superior Court in attempts
to enforce his sweeping exactions. Both of these
summonses proved of no avail, inasmuch as the
Superior Court of Prague disallowed the claims
and the Nuremberg process did not materialize.
In the end the procedure taken against the city
developed into a general annulment of the Jewish
indebtedness, an annulment promulgated by the
King on September 16, 1390. The city of Regensburg was also included in this arrangement, although
it had, in 1385, declined to participate in the general
procedure in relation to the Bavarian claims upon
the Jews. The King finally compelled the reluctant
city to compliance by attaching the goods of Regensburg merchants in the city of Prague. As had been
the case with other cities, the King eventually,
after protracted negotiations, effected an agreement
with Regensburg which provided that in consideration of the payment of a considerable sum, the
amount of which is not known, all the citizens of
Regensburg should be relieved of their indebtedness
to the Jews including, too, such debts as they had
incurred to the Jews in princely territories. The

Jews should retain only such property as they could prove to have purchased. Complaint was made by the Jew Sadia that even his personal silver utensils had been taken from him. That the promise of restitution made to him by the city should be regarded as proof of leniency in the liquidation of Jewish property, is very doubtful.[109] For the city had instituted a house-to-house search among the Jews, and was itself subject to too great a pressure from the King and from those indebted to the Jews to have risked the introduction of any laxity in carrying out their program. The authorities appear, however, to have feared disastrous consequences to the municipal finances in this depredation of Jewish possessions, inasmuch as they remitted to Gnendl the payment of 3000 fl. in consideration of an agreement on his part to remain in the city for two more years and to make an annual payment of 1000 fl. The same interpretation must be put upon a decision by the city in favor of the Jew David, which provided that only 508 fl. of an indebtedness of 600 be remitted, the remaining 92 fl. to remain in force.

The total money losses suffered by the Jews is not known. Gnendl's son, Chalman, was alone the loser of nine bonds of indebtedness totaling 13000 fl. On the death of the wealthy Gnendl in 1391, his widow was unable to continue making the annual payments of 1000 fl. to the city that had been agreed upon. It was ultimately agreed to accept a lump sum of 1450 fl. in lieu of three years' payment of taxes. This too, however, was more than the widow

was able to provide, and she removed for this
reason to Herzogenburg in southern Austria. The
city thereupon appropriated three of the four houses
she possessed in Regensburg.[110]

Out of the money confiscated from the Jews in
1390–91, the Duke received at least 5000 fl., for
which sum a receipt was issued by his commissioner
in May, 1391. With a part of these funds he liquidated, among other obligations, an indebtedness
to his landlord in Passau. The city on its part
established with Gnendl's money an important
institution, the County Court, which it had earlier
been compelled to hypothecate by reason of its
impoverished exchequer. It was also enabled to
repay, with funds obtained from the Jews, municipal obligations of about 3000 fl.

The city had to provide for the return of their
pledges to the debtors of the Jews and to secure
receipts from the latter for the loans which they
had made. It was a wearisome and long-drawn
out affair. Among the final adjustments was the
summary cancellation in 1393 by the Jew Sapsa
of Pappenheim of all his claims against Christians
and Jews in the city of Regensburg.[111]

The King renewed his demands on the Jews in
1394 and 1398, though to a modified extent. In
1394 the Jews of Regensburg were summoned to
appear before the royal tribunal to defend themselves against the charge of having refused to make
the "golden penny offerings" (*goldener opfer-
pfenning*), an obligation which they did not owe,
on account of the pledges given to Bavaria. The

result of this contention is not known. It is probable that negotiations which were held between the King and the city, 1396–97, through the King's chamberlain, and which terminated in a renunciation on the part of the King, on April 8, 1397, were associated with this matter.[112]

In the main, however, the circumstance of the debt cancellation of 1391 satisfied the demands of the King. On September 3, 1391, he issued a Privilege to the Jews by which they were granted greater liberties than those enjoyed by the Jews of other cities. This has reference obviously to state tax exemptions growing out of the pledges given to Bavaria. The King was also satisfied with the agreement he had reached with the city. On February 21, 1392, he confirmed the city's juridical control of the Jews in specific opposition to the ducal tax-levying powers upon them.[113] This was clearly in contravention to the older Bavarian rights, explainable only through the compliant attitude of the reigning dukes, which was shown also on the occasion of the financial demands made by the King upon the Jews. For, immediately following the abdication of King Wenceslaus, dissensions arose between the city and Duke John in the matter of Jewish jurisdiction. On September 13, 1400, Duke John transferred the Jewish jurisdiction to the vidame of lower Bavaria. Similarly, he endeavored to secure for himself an economic advantage from the Jews.[114] There was not much left of the 200 lbs. that had been allocated to him from Jewish taxes. 132 lbs. of this sum had gone

to the city by hypothecation, another 20 lbs. were
pledged to a citizen of Regensburg, 30 lbs. were
owing to the Bishop and more than 7 lbs. were
paid to redeem older indebtedness to Jewish judges
and various functionaries. Of the 200 lbs. there
was left to the Duke only 10 lbs.[115] The former
dukes had been in the habit of furnishing receipts
for such payments. Duke John sought to minimize
his losses by exacting a payment of 1000 fl. for a
Privilege accorded the Jews in 1400. He endeavored
also to negotiate a direct increase in the tax levy
against the Jews, but this attempt was resisted by
the city. Jealousy of the opposite kind had been
manifested at an earlier date by Duke Frederick,
who had reproached the city for having unjustly
raised the tax levy upon the Jews.[116] The city on its
part desired to maintain the jurisdiction of Jewish
affairs which had been granted it, supporting this
contention by the wishes of the Jews themselves,
who must have preferred remaining under the
municipal protectorate, if only by reason of the
fact that they were, in any event, compelled to
reckon with the municipality as the pledge holder
of the greater part of the ducal taxes. It was for
this reason that the city made use of the Jews in its
opposition to the ducal demands, declaring that the
established Jewish right to select their own judge
had been violated by the Duke. Unfortunately,
however, the "unhappy document relating to the
Jewish court" which was to serve as evidence (as
the Council's secretary complains in an entry in
the minutes) was no longer in existence. The matter

was finally decided in favor of the more powerful
party, namely the Duke. In the meantime the
Duke was compelled to relinquish his right when,
in 1401, Rupprecht ascended the throne as King,
and preëmpted for himself the fiscal advantages
connected with the protection of the Jews. Already
in 1401, he confirmed the Jews in their right to
plead in cases of "debt and damage", i. e. in all
money-lending disputes, before the municipal
courts.[117] He reëstablished thereby the dominant
place of the municipality which had been guaranteed by King Wenceslaus's Privilege in 1392. We
shall see in the sequel how after the death of Rupprecht, Duke John again successfully brought
forward his claims to control of Regensburg Jewry.

As regards the Jewish everyday interests, the
municipal administration, through its physical
proximity, constituted a much more important
political factor. When, in 1398, several Jews
attempted to flee the city, taking their capital
with them, they were put under arrest by the city
and upon their liberation compelled to make oath
that they would in future have their cases of Jewish
dispute adjudicated in accordance with Jewry
law, i. e. brought before the *Bet Din*, or, in accordance with "Christian law, before the Jewish magistrate in the Regensburg Court, in line with the
custom of the city", in other words, not according
to the ducal pronouncements. Such action was
taken in the cases of Hamel, i. e. the wife of Chalman, Meister Samuel and his relatives, and Sadya
and his wife Disslaba.[118] The removal of capital

by the Jews is indicated by the fact that the *Hoch-meister* Samuel, of Venice, took all his available property from Regensburg, transferring it to his son Mosse in Eichstätt (1398).

To the degree in which the Jews became impoverished and their dependence upon the municipality rendered ineffectual by the King and the Duke, their value to the city was lost. This decline in their importance to the community brought to the fore elements inimical to the Jews, such as were represented by the smaller tradespeople of the city. As early as July 17, 1393, a legislative decree prohibited Jewish participation in trade. This prohibition was renewed in 1402.[119] It is thus indicated that the Jews had been engaged in commerce, but it is doubtful whether this participation dates back to the customs ordinance of about 1365 which, together with other circumstances, had led us to the inference that Jews had been permitted to engage anew in commercial activities.[120] It is more probable that the dangers associated with the money-lending business which had been intensified by the incidents following 1385, together with the diminution of Jewish capital, had diverted Jewish activities to channels of trade. It is unlikely that this could imply anything but mere attempts at new and short-lived undertakings. The authorities also began to take critical cognizance of the money-lending business. As early as December 8, 1392, the maximum rate of interest of 43 ⅓%—on small and short time loans, 86 ⅔%,[121]—was decided upon as an annual rate, thus enforcing the

customary limits. A higher interest rate must
therefore have previously prevailed in Regensburg,
as is usual in times of disturbance, and it is probable
that this was not unwelcome to the city as it served
to augment its exchequer. In 1402 this tax abatement was again enacted and it was ordered at the
same time that Christians who invested capital
in Jewish money-lending business were to be subjected to the same treatment as the Jews.[122] There
can be no doubt that there existed a strong temp-
tation to continue with the aid of Christian funds
this money-lending business in which the Jews had
suffered extensive losses of capital. In 1405 a loan
was again made to the Duchess Margarete of
Bavaria by Veivelin, the widow of the wealthy
Veivel. Was she still (or again) able to do this
from her private resources? This is possible, but
it was just the wealthy Jews who had been bled
the most. It is not unlikely that there was, especially
in transactions of this nature, a participation of
Christian capitalists.

Still other municipal decrees of this period give
evidence of the fact that the prosperous days of
the Jews were a thing of the past. The prohibition
of exchanging Amberg money had to be sworn to
by Christians as well as Jews as late as 1394.[123]
This had by 1402 become of little consequence to
the Jews, as they were forbidden to engage in money
changing anyhow. At the same time it was directed
that only Christian women over 50 years of age
could be engaged as servants by Jews, especially
as nurses; and an older ordinance was renewed to

the effect that Jews must wait with their purchases
in the fish market on Fridays until after the Christians had been served. These restrictions reveal the
reaction in the status of Jewish living conditions.
The condition of the Jews of Regensburg during
the ensuing seven decades was not subjected to
serious disturbances, but their lives grew steadily
more embittered. There is no authoritative record
of a Jewish persecution in the year 1428.[124] The
report to this effect is probably based upon a
misunderstanding, as is also the information that
after the death of King Sigmund in 1437, a princely
claimant to the throne had been kept in hiding in
the dwelling of a Regensburg Jew.[125] A description
of the magnificence of a rabbinical residence in that
period may also be relegated to the realm of fable.

After 1392 the municipal policy that favored the
Jews became transformed into a policy of restriction.
At the same time the Jews retained a sufficient
importance to provoke the city, the dukes and the
King to continue in uninterrupted strife regarding
their respective rights of levying taxes upon them.
Only when, in the fifth decade of the 15th century,
the Jews became more and more impoverished and
were in continually increasing measure subjected to
clerical persecutions, did the restrictive policy reach
the phase of Jewish expulsion. This development
will be outlined in the following pages.

Shortly after his accession to the throne,
September 4, 1401, King Rupprecht (1401–1410),
confirmed their liberties to the citizens of
Regensburg and received for this concession the

sum of 760 fl., of which 60 fl. was for the personnel
of the Chancery.[126] Dissensions arose in the matter
of the "golden penny offering", which Rupprecht
had also demanded from the Regensburg Jews. The
King, finally, in consideration of the pledge to
Bavaria, rescinded his claim.[127] On the other hand,
the King took steps to obtain new revenue from
the Jews by appointing a chief magistrate for the
Jews of the entire realm, investing him with power
to impose money fines. Judicial authority over the
Jews of the city was also vested in the Jewish
Meister, Israel of Nuremberg. It was his purpose to
establish there a board of four representatives. The
city and the Duke regarded the appointment of
Israel as intrenching upon their own rights of
jurisdiction over the Jews. The Jews on their part,
resisted this appointment as an encroachment upon
their religious affairs. Associated with the King in
these transactions were the vidame of Amberg, the
Bishop of Speyer, the court steward Count of
Oettingen, and the court secretary Kirchen. The
Regensburg interests were placed in the hands of
the Burgomaster Nothaft. The city forbade the
Jews to submit themselves to the decisions of
Israel, as this would impair its jurisdiction over
them. A similar appeal to the King in this matter,
dated February 1, 1408, was disallowed by him and
the city was penalized in the sum of 100 fl. on the
charge of disobedience.[128] There were also negotiations between the Jews and the municipal
authorities. There is still in existence a draft
submitted by the Jews requesting a royal authoriza-

tion relieving them of subordination to the decisions
of Israel. The style of the draft was awkward, as
was the case in those days with most of the
Regensburg Jewish documents in the German
language. The contention is said to have gone so
far that in 1409 the Jews were forbidden even to
accept the written notifications directed to them by
Israel. There does not appear to have been a
paucity of such communications, for in the case of
a single dispute—involving the prominent Jewish
Veiflin family—there was a voluminous inter-
change of letters. Among the members of this
family—the mother, five sons, and two sons-in-
law—who were money-lenders on a large scale,
there arose a dispute in the course of which
reciprocal charges of peculation appear to have been
brought by them.[129] It is not known whether
Israel injected himself as a judge in this process or
whether it was only his purpose to exercise a
punitive police function. In any event he levied a
fine of 20 fl. and a fine consisting of "candles and
lights", as was customary.[130] He had apparently
made a larger demand originally, for he was
enjoined by the King (March 17, 1408) to content
himself with 20 fl. The fact that there had been an
exchange of letters in this matter between Count
Oettingen, the court secretary, and the city, would
indicate that it was not only a matter of finance
but that fundamental political interests were
involved. This fine had not been paid by the
beginning of 1409. It is probable that the issue
came to nothing, inasmuch as the post held by

Israel was abolished upon the death of the King (1410).

Other political entanglements are revealed in the fate of the Veiflin family. In connection with a dispute with the Jewish community, the Veiflins with their five sons (Michel, Sanwel, Isaac, Mosse, Jössel), as being the wealthiest of the Jews, were sentenced (May 25, 1411) to defray one-half of the entire Jewish taxes.[131] In consideration of this payment, Jössel was given a prominent place in the direction of the community and was to have a voice in all its transactions excepting those relating to tax levies. The wealth of the before-mentioned Michel is said to have subsequently led to a similar procedure in Straubing. He was placed under arrest in that city in 1419 and compelled to make his home there. On April 23, 1422, Michel of Straubing, as he was thereafter styled, was accorded an extraordinarily valuable Privilege by Duke John, which was characterized in the main by the authority vested in Michel in his relation to the other Jews of Straubing. Influence in all internal Jewish affairs was guaranteed him by the Duke, but he was exempted from all special imposts levied upon the Jews. Notable, too, is the privilege accorded him in the matter of procedural law. In the manner of the older provision, he could be convicted only on the testimony of both Christian and Jewish witnesses. It is evident that in this period of the Council of Basle and the war of the

Hussites, Jewish money—and, at any rate, the wealthy Jews,—were again accorded special consideration.

As Duke John had accepted as subject the Jew Michel, so had other rulers accepted other Regensburg Jews. The city was no longer able to hold them. It was the same policy of inviting Jews to their domains that had formerly been adopted by the city, but in the opposite direction. In 1412, the Jew Salomon became in this manner obligated to the bishopric of Passau, and in 1410, Jonas, who had resided in Regensburg only since 1408, to the Archbishop of Mayence. The Bavarian dukes took the Regensburg Jews under their immediate care, notably Duke Henry the Rich. The city also, on its part, accepted as subjects new Jewish citizens, as for example, in 1409, Hoschel of Pilsen,[132] although in this case the invitation to new Jews was less purposeful and less persistent than had been the case several decades before.

In the conflict over the profitable Jewish control, the Bavarian Duke, following the death of King Rupprecht, again entered the lists against the rivalry of the city. Following a number of disputes, an agreement was reached on November 3, 1410, in which the city was completely subordinated. The Duke was to receive an annual sum of 200 lbs. for a period of 15 years, and the city only 60 lbs.; the more important legal fees were to be shared, and jurisdiction in the lesser ones to remain in the hands of the ducal Jewish magistrate. At the same time a protective decree for the Jews was promulgated by the Duke in which he emphasized his sole control of all matters relating to the Jews. The latter were compelled to pay 1000 lbs. for this Privilege, which sum had to be advanced by the city. This money was to be repaid by the Jews in two yearly installments.[133] The Duke made energetic use of his rights himself or through his vidame in Straubing, because he was away the greater part of the time. He was at the same time bishop of Lüttich, where he was styled *Jean sans pitié*. In 1414 he appointed a citizen of Regensburg, Peter Mäller, as Jewish magistrate.[134] In 1421 he made a special tax levy of 8000 fl. upon the Jews to defray the expenses of a campaign against the Hussites, of which sum 4000 fl. had actually to be paid.[135] To enforce the ducal demands, the vidame came to Regensburg with a cavalcade of 82 horsemen and, placing the Jews under arrest, entered into negotiations with them over a period of four days.[136] This incident makes it clear that the amount of this levy strained the financial capacity of the Jews and that the city was entirely subordinate to the Duke.

In the reign of King Sigmund, when the imperial power was once more placed upon a strong foundation (1414–37), the Duke, too, was again forced to abandon his authoritative position. On July 30, 1414, the new King confirmed their privileges to the Regensburg Jews in the traditional manner.[137] There is no record of a payment being made by the Jews on this occasion, but it is to be presumed that such was made. Within six months of his accession (January 7, 1415), the King, as an offset to this confirmation of Regensburg Jewish rights, levied a special tax not only upon the Jews of that city but upon all other Jews of Lower Bavaria, i. e. in the domain of Duke John, to defray the costs of his Italian campaign.[138] The Duke gave his approval to this special tax levy and declared he would not hold the city financially liable.[139] The declaration indicates that there must have been negotiations before the approval was given. When, in 1421, the Duke forcibly exacted the payment of those 4000 fl., the King complained that he had gotten the worst of the bargain (*"zu kurz gekommen"*) and rescinded a previous declaration to the effect that he would forgo all claims against the Jews of Regensburg until the Duke had given his assent. After the death of this energetic Duke (1425), the King proceeded to adopt stronger methods. On February 16, 1425, he issued, through the Count Palatine John, a summons against the Jews on a charge of disobedience, at the same time directing the Bishop to forbid Christians to have any trade relations with the Jews so long as the latter continued recalcitrant. Dukes Ernest and William of Munich, as inheritors of the Bavarian Jewish pledges,[140] supported the Jews in their opposition to the royal demands. Nothing is known regarding the issue of this contention with the King. The dukes of Munich renewed, on September 9, 1427, the customary Regensburg Jewish Privilege, and appointed as Jewish magistrate the citizen Erhard Reich.

In 1429, consequent upon a new division of the
provinces among the ducal cousins, the Regensburg
pledge ownership was acquired by the Ingolstadt
Duke Louis, the maniacal bully who was subsequently cast into prison by his own son and
perished miserably. He, too, renewed the Jewish
liberties (July 1, 1429), the Jews promising in
consideration therefor to make biennial payments
of their delinquent taxes in four installments
(1430–36).[141] Duke Louis, with an energy inherited
from his forbears, the Italian bankers Visconti,
engaged upon a consistent exploitation of the Jews.
He appointed, in addition to the Bailiff (chief
magistrate) Conrad Gräfenreuter, the Jews Nasse
of Ingolstadt and the Regensburg Meister (Rabbi?)
Anshelm as Jewish magistrates (June 27, 1429).[142]
A closer examination reveals the fact that these
measures were intelligently considered. The
inclusion of the Bailiff in this magistracy indicates
that a previous understanding had been reached
with the city, at any rate that the interests of the
municipality were to be given consideration. The
appointment of the Jew Nasse, who as resident of
the ducal capital Ingolstadt stood in high favor
with the Duke, as associate of the Regensburg rabbi,
indicates an intention to satisfy also the desires of
the Jews. The assumption is not unlikely that the
ducal interests in matters of Jewish admission and
taxation were looked after by Nasse and that
Anshelm was entrusted with collecting the legal
fees in internal Jewish matters. As both nominations
are known to us only through transcripts of the

records, it is possible that the appointment of
Anselm had only been considered. At any rate
Nasse entered upon official duties, his name
appearing as Jewish *Hochmeister* in an arbitration
case of April 7, 1435.[143] No less energetic were the
methods adopted by Duke Louis in opposing
claims against the Jews by other persons. Without
apparent reason he resisted the age-old claim of the
Bishop to a share of 30 lbs. of the Jewish tax
revenues. The quarrel that ensued was decided by
the Emperor in favor of the Bishop after much
argument (April 11, 1431), in the course of which
the Jews also, who had been called as witnesses in
the matter, testified in favor of the Bishop as
supported by the former practice.[144]

In the meantime the Emperor, too, sought to
secure further revenues from the Jews. He renewed
his demand that the Bishop prohibit trading with
Jews by Christians until the former showed
themselves complaisant. The Bishop, in his
embarrassment, turned to the Munich dukes for aid,
asking them to use their influence with the Jews.[145]
Not that the Munich dukes were the competent
authority in this matter, but the Bishop shared
with them their common attitude of antagonism
to Duke Louis, the factual overlord of the Jews.
It appears that the Bishop was in the end compelled
to comply with the Emperor's command, as there
is in existence a letter of appeal to the Pope, signed
by Christian citizens, in which they protested
against the excommunication decreed by the
Bishop.[146] Inasmuch, however, as this letter exists

only in the form of a rough draft, it is possible
that it was never forwarded and that it reflected
apprehensions of the appellants rather than actual
occurrences.

The unequivocal recognition of the ecclesiastical
claims upon Jewish imposts was an entirely new
phase in the affairs of Regensburg. These circumstances are explainable by the reform tendencies of
the times, which included a desire to see the
ecclesiastical interests again in control of the
Jewish community. The city of Regensburg resisted
the intrusion in its affairs of a new authoritative
factor, namely the Church, as encroaching upon
matters in which it desired to exercise its own rule.
There was revealed for the first time, even though
not clearly, an inclination to expel the Jews, whose
presence was of little advantage to the city but
presented many phases of trouble and annoyance.
In the above-mentioned letter of appeal, the town
clerk suggests that intercourse with the Jews could
not be broken off as was demanded by the Bishop,
so long as they remained in the city, but that it
would not be difficult to induce them to depart of
their own accord.[147] The city served as buffer for
the contending claims of the King and the Bishop
and faced continual unpleasantness on account of
the Jews. To this was added the disillusionment
occasioned by the overthrow of its own claims upon
the Jews. These municipal pretensions were
gradually relinquished during the 15th century,
owing to the continued and permanent decay of the
city's economic development. Thus there dis-

appeared in the course of time the expectations
held by the city of securing substantial advantages
from the Jews that would offset the considerable
unpleasantness associated with their presence. The
situation was eased with the death of the
obstreperous Duke Louis in 1447. The Regensburg
Jewish control came into the hands of his cousin
Duke Henry—also a scion of the Visconti banking
family—an avaricious man, who is also described
as a shrewd businessman and who is reproached
by the chronicler as having been too much devoted
to deer-stalking and to the Jews.[148]

In the meantime the Jews of Regensburg would
in any event have been almost lost to the control
of the Bavarian house in 1434. Duke Louis had
fallen under the Imperial ban and the Emperor
declared the Jews subservient to the Empire. He
directed the President of the Imperial Exchequer
to have the Jews turned over to his jurisdiction.[149]
The city was threatened, in the event of opposition,
with the Imperial ban and with ecclesiastical
excommunication by the Council of Basle. Shortly
before this, the Jews had been summoned to appear
before the Council of Basle, where an assessment
of 1400 fl. was levied against them. As it was
impossible to collect this sum, the Emperor exacted
an advance in this amount from the President of
the Exchequer, giving him an assignment upon the
Regensburg Jews. The Emperor himself eventually
came to Regensburg, and the Jews were unable to
evade his personal demand upon them. The contention again resulted in a compromise. The Jews,

as an offset to the payment made by them, received, on September 15, 1434, a royal Privilege confirming their former liberties, but including the following new provisions:—that the Jews be permitted to loan money at interest; that they be accorded redemption claims for money loaned upon pledges of stolen property; that they be not compelled to submit to trial by ordeal; that they be summoned for trial only before tribunals composed of an equal number of Jewish and Christian judges; and that the assessments imposed upon them be not increased.[150] These provisions proved of distinct advantage to the Jews, but ran counter, in their conservative trend, to the spirit of the reform period, and never became operative. At the same time the Emperor renounced his demand for the reversion of the Jews to the Empire and recognized the fundamental right of continued Bavarian Jewish control. Nevertheless the tax payment by the Jews was protested by the outlawed Duke Louis. It was not the Emperor's ultimate intention, however, to renounce the reversion of the Jews, inasmuch as in the above-mentioned Privilege of 1434 it was distinctly provided that in the event of its violation by any one of the dukes, control of the Jews should revert to the Emperor.

It turned out shortly thereafter that the assignment given the President of the Imperial Exchequer for the advance made by him on the Jewish tax levy had not been paid. The Council of Basle itself, on February 28, 1435, made a demand upon the city of Regensburg to exact payment of this levy from the Jews. There is no record, however, as to the result of this demand.

With the death of King Sigmund in 1437 the influence of the Council, which had been established at his suggestion, came to an end. His successor, Albrecht II, had already in 1421 expelled the Jews from his city of Vienna. Upon his accession he levied, through Jewish intermediaries, a property tax of $33\frac{1}{3}\%$ upon all the Jews of the realm. Of this tax there was imposed upon the Jews of Regensburg a sum of only 4000 fl., indicating that the entire valuation of their possessions did not exceed 12,000 fl. The decline in the wealth of the Jews is thus shown to have been considerable, when it is remembered that at the time of the second cancellation of Jewish debts under King Wenceslaus[151] a single one of their number had been able to relinquish letters of indebtedness for 13,000 fl.

Following the premature death of Albrecht, the throne was occupied by King Frederick III, a man who in the latter period of his reign exercised a significant influence upon the destiny of the Jews of Regensburg. He demanded shortly after his accession, as had his predecessors, the customary mark of honor from the Regensburg Jews (July 28, 1442).[152] He does not appear to have received this pledge of loyalty until August 20, 1444, as his decree confirming the Jews in their established rights bears this date.[153] This Privilege was renewed in 1464, following the acquiescence of Duke Louis the Rich, the holder of the Jewish pledges, in a tax levy by Frederick upon the Jews at the time of the

declaration of peace in Prague in 1463.[154] In 1474
the Emperor demanded the sum of 4000 fl. from
the Jews for the prosecution of his war with
Burgundy. The city and the Jews again, as they
had in former times, protested this assessment, in
view of the Bavarian pledges. The Emperor
threatened them with the Imperial ban and
despatched a personal legation to Regensburg.[155]
The demand was finally lost sight of in the troubles
that broke upon the Regensburg Jews in 1476.
The demands made upon the Jews by Frederick
were less frequent than had been those made by
Sigmund. This is to be attributed in the main to
the impoverished condition into which the Jews
had fallen.[156]

Duke Henry, who had in 1447 taken over the
pledges connected with the Regensburg Jewish
control, issued on March 13, 1447 a guarantee of
protection to them covering a period of eight years,
in line with previous custom. His son and successor,
Duke Louis, who came to the throne upon the death
of his father in 1450, drove the Jews out of Southern
Bavaria shortly after his accession. He had
developed a strong opposition to his father, and
adopted a pronounced anti-Jewish policy, although
he, on his part, also extended the guarantee of
protection to the Regensburg Jews for eight-year periods, 1450, 1458, 1466, 1474. The Jews made regular
payments of 1000 to 2000 fl. in consideration of
these guarantees. In 1452 he made urgent demands
upon the city that it give greater care to the
carrying out of the ecclesiastical regulations

regarding the Jewish garb. Later, in 1474, he
ordered the delivery of sermons for the proselytizing
of the Jews, which they were compelled to attend
and, finally, is reported to have actively participated
in the ritual-murder-charge mania with which the
Jews were harried in 1476. At about this time
there was issued by the supreme head of the Church,
Pope Nicholas V, a papal bull of toleration in
favor of the Jews of Upper Germany (September
20, 1451), which was also promulgated on
November 20, 1452, for the ecclesiastical province
of Salzburg, of which Regensburg formed a part.[157]

The fact that the protector of the Jews of
Regensburg had expelled the Jews from his own
domain of Lower Bavaria reacted also upon the
situation of the former. One of their most important
guarantees, the right to have their legal disputes
brought before the Jewish tribunal in Regensburg,
a right which had been secured to them in every
Privilege, was now endangered. Trials of a number
of charges brought against the Jews of Regensburg
were brought before courts outside of the city.
Judgments and executions against the Jews would
have involved not only the Jews, but the city
itself, in most disastrous consequences. It is therefore understandable that the Jews commissioned
the municipal functionaries to represent them
before the courts. It is to be credited to the
influence exerted by the city that the Bavarian
Dukes in 1452 and 1454 directed their provincial
courts to dismiss the cases brought against the
Regensburg Jews.[158] The city also countered

attempts that were made to bring the Jews for
trial before the Westphalian vehmic court and
ecclesiastical tribunals by throwing insistent
plaintiffs into prison.[159]

In this fashion the city furnished protection to
the Jews insofar as its own interests were affected,
but restricted this protection where the interests
of its citizens or the sentiment of the ecclesiastical
authorities called for it. The municipal guarantees
of protection are preserved from the years 1429,
1439, 1440, 1441, and they provide, in accordance
with the ducal letters of protection, that the city
itself receive annually 60 lbs., the dukes 200 lbs.,
out of the Jewish revenues. This municipal
guarantee, similarly with that of the dukes, was as
late as 1429 extended over eight-year periods.[160]
After 1439—probably since 1437, that is at the
conclusion of the eight-year term which began with
1429—the renewal of these guarantees was limited
to a period of one year, though in 1441 it was
once more extended to two years.[161] When one
considers the extension of this term, which since
1376 had grown from a two to three year period
to one of eight years, and which was eventually in
1439 restricted to a single year, one can recognize
the beginning of the diminishing interest of the
municipality, the reasons for which have been
outlined in the foregoing. The persecutory activities
of the captain of the town militia in the year 1439,
above referred to, are also thus explainable,
although these were deeply rooted in purely personal
interests.[162]

The tendency toward the adoption of greater restrictive measures against the Jews, together with the antagonism engendered by the invasion of the "unbelieving" Turks, was intensified with the arrival in Regensburg of such crusading preachers as Giovanni Capistrano and Heinrich Kalteisen. The former had already in the previous year (1353) taken an active part in the Jewish persecutions in Breslau. His devastating exhortations heightened the tense social and religious animosities of the time. The municipality had already in 1452 forbidden the functioning of Christian midwives for Jewish women. In 1463, Jews were punished for conducting business at Easter time. New restrictive measures were adopted in 1456 and 1459 in connection with Jewish purchases in the fish market. In 1461 admission to the city was restricted by the exclusion of "Jewish brides" from other localities. In 1462 it was decreed that Christian citizens should no longer act as sureties for Jews. An order was issued in 1475 that Jews be accorded their legal rights as before and that they should be privileged to petition the Bishop in cases of antagonism on the part of the clergy, at the same time, however, requesting the Emperor to "eliminate the Jews" or at least to restrict the right of ownership in purchased goods which had been stolen— in line with the regulations on this subject in force in Ulm and Nuremberg. Mention should be made in this connection of the municipal enactments of 1462 and 1471 concerning the obligation of Jews to appear with fire apparatus at the

approaching session of the Diet.[163] Evidences of
the impoverished condition of the Jewish community, to which reference has been made as existing
in the third decade, are also found in the sixties,
the Jews being shown to have been delinquent in
the payment of their regular yearly taxes.

A degeneration of the Jewish banking business in
Regensburg to the lending of money to poor people
for consumption must have occurred at about this
time. It is clear that the character of the business
formerly carried on by the Jews could have been
conducted only on the basis of large capital. Small
resources could not have enabled them to engage
in anything but the advancing of loans on pledges.
Added to this, with the economic decadence of the
city, the citizen of small means was the first to be
compelled to go to the Jews to raise a few farthings.
Up to the fifties there is no evidence of extended
pledge loaning activities on the part of the Jews,
and promissory notes indicating larger loans and
credits are also non-existent.

The increasing number of reports of the degeneration of Jewish morals also points to the desolate
condition of the Jews. One may mention in this
connection the malignant agitation against Israel
of Brünn (J. Bruna).[164] Frequently Jews were
punished under the influence of ecclesiastical
legislation for sexual relations with Christian
women.[165] The legal punishment for this offense was
death, but in practice the penalty was brief imprisonment or a money fine. In 1447 two wandering Jewish students (*Schalantjuden*)[166] were punished for

resisting the police. In 1450 a Jew was punished
for forging documents, and in another case (1460)
for a threat of murder. In 1474 a Jewish poisoner
was put to death. In 1475 punishment was meted
out to a frequently baptized Jewish adventurer who
is said to have been engaged for many years in
importing *etrogim*.[167] We hear about the same time
of a rascally (*abgefeimten*) Jew who was charged
with being a receiver of stolen goods. Though one
or the other of these incidents may be traced to
judicial errors, which were not infrequent, they are
not in the main to be charged to anti-Jewish
prejudice of the courts. Punishment was also dealt
out to Christians who had committed offenses
against the Jews. There is little evidence of
intense criminal activity of Jews even if full credence
be given to all the reports, but the number of
crimes exceeded that of former times.

An unusual phase of the Jewish economic
existence in this period is recorded in the year 1443,
when the city of Regensburg purchased a new
clock from a Jewish clockmaker and turned the
old clock over to him for repairs.[168] In 1471 the
anti-Semitic Duke Louis asked for the attendance
in Regensburg of a Jewish physician, probably in
view of the approaching "Festival", when there was
to be a large concourse of people in the city.
Mention is made in the same period of a Jewish
physician, Salomon, and his son Josef, also a
physician. The former is probably identical with
the Doctor Salomon Platsch of Regensburg[169] who
had resided in Frankfort-on-the-Main in 1392.

The disturbed living conditions described above were crystalized in 1473 in a letter of grievances against the Jews addressed by the Regensburg clergy to the Pope. The cause that led to this complaint as well as the contents of the letter are not known. A later development indicates that Bishop Henry, known as an implacable fanatic, took umbrage at the usury practiced by the Jews and the existence in Regensburg of a school for the study of the Talmud. And there were actual incidents besides. In 1470 the Jewish cantor Kalman, who had planned to have himself baptized and for this purpose had made his home for some time in the residence of the Suffragan Bishop, was ousted from his post.[170] He returned, however, to the Jewish fold, this act resulting in a public trial in which Duke Louis also participated by appointing as prosecutor Ebran von Wildenberg, a later chronicler. The accused declared at the hearing (May 4) that the "discipline and honor" in the Augustinian Monastery, located in the vicinity of the Jewish quarter, had so impressed him that he had been induced to accept baptism, but that in deference to the pleading of his relatives, and owing to the coarse behavior of the Bishop's servants, had renounced this intention. He also declared on May 6 that the Jews would have murdered him in the event of his baptism as they had done in the case of others, and accused many Jews of Regensburg and other places with having desecrated the Host. One may assume in the face of these conflicting declarations that the accused had been subjected

to the customary torture in the days intervening
between these sessions.[171] A strong impression was
unquestionably made upon the Bishop by the
revelations of this process. The accused was
condemned to death, though the Jews do not
appear to have been subjected to further reprisals,
excepting a financial one, the Jewish community
being compelled to pay a sum of 100 fl. to the
Duke in order to avoid further complications.[172]
The incident, however, had a repercussion in
giving ready credence to the ritual-murder charge
lodged by the converted Jew Veyol against Israel of
Brünn in 1474. The latter was placed under arrest
and released only upon the intervention of the
Emperor and the King of Bohemia. The city
compelled the converted Jew to withdraw his
accusation and he was condemned to death.

If already in the case of Kalman in 1470 the
economic interests had been brought forward in
addition to the religious and juridical influences,
they were further emphasized in the ritual-murder
charge of 1476, which assumed large proportions.
The Bishop had brought to the attention of the
Duke the fact that in the ritual-murder trial in
Trent, the Jewish convert Wolfgang, one of the
co-defendants, had reported the commission of
similar crimes by Jews of Regensburg. The city,
too, was made acquainted with these charges and
suggested the mode of procedure to the Duke, who,
as being invested with the control of Jewish affairs,
was the competent authority. First they confiscated the Jewish possessions, not only those

belonging to the accused individuals—this would
have accorded with the normal judicial procedure—
but the property of the entire Jewish community.
The city looked above all to securing the houses
owned by the Jews. In the negotiations with the
Duke the city declared its readiness to allow his
right of taxing the Jews if it could retain possession
of their houses. The transaction, however, fell
through, for the Duke dropped the entire matter
when he discovered that the Emperor was strongly
opposed to it. The Bishop, too, withdrew from the
affair, declaring that he had made reference to the
matter merely in the course of conversation and
did not want the Emperor to know anything
about it.[173] The matter might have been concluded
without further consequences, as had been the case
in a similar occurrence in 1474, had it not been for
the insistent contention of the city that the Jews
who had confessed under torture be convicted. The
Emperor sought to avail himself of this opportunity
to secure control of the Regensburg Jewry, an
attempt that had been made by many of his
predecessors and which was finally achieved by his
successor in 1501. This attempt enraged the
municipality, but the decisive factor was that the
city really desired to rid itself of the Jews, and for
good reason. By reason of its economic retrogres-
sion, the city was regarded as overpopulated, and
it was decided by the magistracy in 1485 that no
additional Christian citizens be admitted. The

Burgomaster is reported to have expressed himself
as follows: "My name is not Hans Notscherf if I
fail to destroy the synagogue of the Jews." It was
a deep-seated hatred and could not have been
engendered over night. It brought in its wake the
commission of many unwise acts and led to most
disreputable transactions; strengthening still further
the Emperor's disinclination to come to an agreement with the city. The Emperor finally withdrew
the city's right to inflict the death penalty,
depriving the municipality of the power to punish
serious offences committed within its limits. The
city submitted itself to these restrictions. It
requested only, and was accorded, a moderate
phrasing of these imperial requirements in order to
cloak its humiliation. In addition the Emperor
accorded the city the costs connected with the
Jewish prosecutions, which were to be defrayed by
the Jews with a payment of 10,000 fl. The latter
were also required to turn over to the Emperor a
sum of 8000 fl., in consideration of protection
accorded them, this money to be advanced by the
city. The 17 accused Jews were liberated after
having been held in solitary confinement for 4½
years. The other members of the Jewish community, who had been held in protective custody,
had been set free at a prior date. As the Emperor
was unable immediately to collect the entire sum
of 8000 fl. from the Jews, an agreement was reached
by which annual payments of 200 fl. were to be

made. If the Emperor had not in the end again
secured the control of the Jewish community, he
had at any rate won a permanent claim to the
levying of taxes upon them, a claim that could
easily create a foundation for further demands.

The Emperor had exacted a pledge from the city
that it would not drive out its Jews,[174] even though
they failed to pay to the city the costs of their
prosecution, but at the same time he placed the
city in the position of acting as trustee of his own
demands upon the Jews, by the requirement that
the Jews be kept in the city until their indebtedness
had been liquidated. The plan of expulsion was
thus rendered inoperative for the immediate future
and the city was advised to defer the expulsion of
the Jews until after the death of the Emperor.
This plan was actually carried out following the
death of the next Emperor (1519). The enforced
retention of the Jews in the city served to intensify
the animosity against them, the more so as the
impoverishment suffered by them in consequence of
their four years of imprisonment had become
aggravated and had made it impossible for them for
a period of years to meet the new assessments
levied against them, which in fact were never paid.

For it was especially the wealthy Jews who were
most desperately affected, notably the head of the
community, Jössel, who in 1476 had been indicted
as the principal offender.

The protection, too, which was accorded the
Jews from outside sources served only to their
disadvantage in their relations with the city. Some

individual Jews had managed to secure protection from a number of nobles of the Upper Palatinate and Bohemia. The negotiations with the city in the matter of its refusal to release the Jews and their property resulted in occasional threats of conflict. In the case of entirely impecunious Jews, the city was willing to come to terms. The final four decades of the Regensburg Jewry are replete with serious political and economic distresses of the city, and these, too, exerted unfavorable influence upon the condition of the Jews.

The death of Duke Louis occurred in the course of these happenings (1479). His successor, Duke George, occupied an entirely different position in relation to the Regensburg Jews. The political situation had been left unchanged by the Emperor, but he had drawn to himself the practical control of the Jewish community and had claimed authority, in association with the city, over the entire taxable resources of the Jews. There was nothing left for the Duke but occasional attempts to secure revenues through Jewish taxation and to regain jurisdiction over their legal affairs. All these attempts on his part proved futile. Jewish jurisdiction was not in any event reëstablished after its disruption at the time of the imprisonment of the Jews. Later attempts to revive it, notably in the reign of Maximilian I, proved equally ineffectual through lack of planning initiative and intensive effort. The city obstructed these attempts and transferred the functions of the disbanded Jewish court to the regular municipal courts.

The transfer of the Jewish control from ducal to imperial domination received a temporary check when in 1486 the municipality was compelled by reason of its impoverishment to dispose of its freedom to Duke Albrecht. By this action the latter acquired the jurisdiction over the Jews which had previously been vested in the city. As, however, the scope of this jurisdiction had never been clearly defined in relation to the rights inherited by Duke George, complications arose anew in the constitutional status of the Jews. Duke Albrecht eventually made an effort to purchase the Jewish control from his cousin. This plan, however, failed to materialize, as the Emperor had in the meantime reconfirmed to the city its autonomous status, thus overriding the claims of Duke Albrecht in the matter of the Regensburg Jewish control. The matter was simplified when, after the death of Duke George, in 1503, and the ensuing War of Succession, the Emperor acquired control of the Regensburg Jews as well as other Bavarian possessions.

The interest of the rulers in Jewish affairs retained its purely fiscal character. The dukes, especially Albrecht, endeavored to discover the value of Jewish property for tax purposes through local informants.[175] Belief in their wealth still prevailed. This was certainly not the case in any general sense, although there were individual instances of prosperity among the Jews despite the city's general economic decline. The prevailing impoverishment led, however, to discord with the city as well as within the Jewish community itself.

Within the modest scope to which their efforts
were restricted the Jews had not resigned themselves
to forgo attempts at improving their condition.
During the persecutions of 1476–80, they too, had
maintained a representation at the imperial court.
The name of their representative was Süssel, and
when the city of Regensburg learned in 1477 that
there had been a reported desecration of the Host
in the neighborhood of Passau, it endeavored to
involve him in the matter in order to render his
influence innocuous. As this was impossible by
reason of his absence, his son was placed under
arrest. In this case, too, the Emperor had to
interfere and compel his release. On the other
hand, the Emperor also maintained a Jewish
delegation in Regensburg in order to negotiate the
matter of the protective imposts due him by the
imprisoned Jews (1478). His representative was
the "Imperial Jew David of Nuremberg".

Repressive measures against the Jews were
greatly augmented after the end of the 80's, and
they sent, as did the city, frequent delegations to
the Duke at Landshut. At first their complaints
were directed against changes in their juridical and
economic affairs. These included disruption of the
Jewish court, economic restrictions, and illegal tax
levies. After the 90's they complained in addition
that the city failed to protect them against outrages
and personal assaults. In 1493 there was an uprising
in Regensburg which gave a temporary ascendancy
to the people's party, which was antagonistic to
the Jews. This faction, however, proved itself

incapable of carrying on the governmental
functions.[176] Responsibility for the attacks on the
Jews was laid at its door. At the same time discord
manifested itself anew among the Jews. In 1497
the Jews themselves enacted a decree proposed by
the ten members of the Council (*Sitzer*) and
attested by the Rabbis Anschel (or Oscher) and
David, imposing penalties upon persons guilty of
acts of violence.[177] The Jews, too, became
demoralized by the prevailing distress and violent
dissensions were frequent among them regarding
matters of taxation. Many individual protests were
registered with the city authorities by taxpayers
against the unjust assessments levied by those in
charge of the Jewish taxes. Duke George made
occasional efforts to reorganize the method of
taxation and in 1488 commissioned the Jews Mair
and Anshelm to formulate a new tax regulation. It
was the practice to deposit the Jewish tax payments
in a chest, the key to which was in possession of
the tax officials. This method apparently was not
properly carried out and it was proposed that while
the chest be kept in the hands of the tax officials,
the key be transferred to the Beadle.[178] This may
afford an explanation of the peculiar incident in
1494, when the Emperor Maximilian directed,
without consulting the Jews, that the function
exercised by the Beadle be turned over to Abraham
von Aysch.[179]

Another evidence of the demoralized condition of
the Jews is found in a statement made by Antonius
Margherita, the converted son of the Regensburg

Rabbi, in which he charges that the "rich Mosse",
whose family is designated as "Wölfe", had
maligned the Jews to the imperial captain, who had,
in consequence, subjected all of them to payments
of fines. Though this deponent may not be entirely
trustworthy, his information in this matter may, in
the light of the above recorded happenings, be
given credence. He reports further that the Jews
could have prevented their expulsion if they had
not been in disagreement among themselves.

This assumption is unquestionably erroneous,
inasmuch as the conditions that prevailed in the
city, in which another revolution had broken out
in 1513 costing the lives of several of the returning
municipal patricians, had grown increasingly tense.
It is certain, however, that had there been a greater
unity among the Jews there might have been
brought about a cancellation of the old tax delinquencies and therewith a more propitiatory spirit, and
the various attempts on the part of the dukes and
the Emperor to compound the existing differences
would have been made easier.

The imposts demanded by the city and the Duke
had not been paid for several decades. This was
true also of the 10,000 fl. owing to the Emperor—
and in reversion to the city—since the year
1478. Regarding this latter sum the Jews disputed
among themselves, the later newcomers and those
who had since grown to maturity maintaining that
only the signatories, of whom some had died in the
meantime, were liable for the debt. Conditions
were reversed, inasmuch as the Jews who had

formerly enjoyed a continued protection which they could purchase were now held in general disfavor by reason of their refusal to make such payments. The efforts of the Duke and the Emperor to ameliorate the strained relations existing between the citizens and the Jews were actuated too largely by a spirit of superficial opportunism to achieve any practical results. In 1488, at the instigation of the Duke, a diet was convoked in Landshut for the purpose of conciliating the two factions. In 1493, 1500 and 1513, imperial commissioners[180] were sent to the city for the purpose of restoring peace in the municipality generally and at the same time to regulate the condition of the Jews. As these efforts proved fruitless, the Emperor finally directed the Innsbruck administration to take charge of the affair and bring it to a conclusion either by amicable means or, in the event of failure, by legal process. The law suit brought by the city against the Jews, which lasted from 1516 to 1519, resulted in a decision favorable to the Jews, the city being ordered to reëstablish their former legal status which had, however, proven untenable. This decision, although favorable to the Jews, resulted— as had the aid given them by the Emperor (1476–80)—disastrously for them. The city took advantage of the Interregnum which followed upon the death of Maximilian to bring about a *fait accompli*, and in February, 1519, expelled the Jews from its territory. After some preliminary hesitation the imperial government finally yielded. A portion of their confiscated property, altogether

only 4750 fl., was returned to the Jews—one of
the Jewish attorneys in this liquidation being the
son of the wealthy Mosse, of the family of
"Wölfe"—but the decree of expulsion was not
rescinded. The "Jew money" however (i. e. the
Jewish taxes), the city had to pay to the Emperor
until well into the 18th century.

From this period of Jewish impoverishment there
date the pawnshop certificates, which reveal that
the Jews continued to be the creditors of common
people only, and that the larger scale money-
lending business had entirely ceased. That this
was a fact and is not merely a lacuna in the records
of the time, is revealed in a complaint made by
the Jewish magistrate, in the eighties, that no
bonds of indebtedness were being registered or
executed. The general economic condition of the
Jews was a pitiful one and the economic distress
of the poorer classes, i. e. the debtors of the Jews,
was bound to result in disastrous consequences
for the latter. There existed, however, in those
days, isolated instances of larger money-lending
transactions, although only three bankers are
recorded as being identified with these loans.[181]

That the prevailing distress reacted so unfavor-
ably upon the Jews was due in large measure to
incitements by special agitators of popular passions
and the influence of political leaders. At the time
of the Jewish persecutions of 1476–80, a nobleman
named Fuchssteiner deliberately intrigued against
the Jews. He is known from the historical annals

of the municipality as a dangerous political agitator.[182] In this period, also, the Christian clergy entered the arena as a bitter enemy of the Jews. In the nineties it became customary for the preachers in the cathedral to incite the people against the Jews. There can be no doubt that this attitude was influenced, too, by sympathy with the economic distress of the impoverished citizens and the ecclesiastical opposition to the practice of money-lending at interest. The anti-Semitism of the fanatical preacher, Balthasar Hubmaier, who was himself, in 1526, executed on the charge of ana-baptism, was undoubtedly sincere. He was one of the outstanding factors in the campaign for Jewish expulsion. Owing to his heretical pulpit pronounce-ments he was on various occasions commanded by the Emperor to leave the city. A Papal Bull against Jewish usury had been launched in 1512 through the efforts of Johannes, the administrator of the bishopric. This Papal interdiction was renewed in 1517, but the administrator was prevented by the Emperor's orders from putting it into effect.[183]

Together with the manifold causes that led to the Jewish expulsion there must also be taken into consideration the important material interests involved. In the same manner as, behind the Jewish persecutions of 1476, there was the desire to acquire Jewish houses cheaply, so in 1519 there was an economic interest in driving out the Jews. It is reported by the contemporary Jewish magistrate himself that there were a number who were opposed to the plan of Jewish expulsion, as "not many

sacks" would be necessary to hold the money of
the Jews.

The Jewish persecutions were also stigmatized as
unjust. But these opinions could not find public
expression in view of the aggressive popular sentiment that prevailed. To forestall any possible
interference, the intention to expel the Jews was
kept secret and the victims were given only three
days' notice to liquidate their property. This term
was ultimately extended to eight days. When news
of the event reached the Innsbruck administration,
the solicitor of the Jews, Johannes Zasius (Zisar),
was despatched to Regensburg to prevent the
carrying out of this outrage, but he came too late.

The circumstances above referred to indicate that
there were among the residents of Regensburg some
who were not inimical to the Jews. Many of the
latter who had found refuge in the Bavarian
Stadtamhof, only about one kilometer distant,
continued their business relations with citizens of
Regensburg, which the city found itself repeatedly
called upon to interdict. In 1543, an effort was
made by the Jews to legalize such business relations,
pointing out that the right of the city to keep out
the Jews applied only to continued residence, but
not to occasional coming and going. Before this
contention could be threshed out, the Jews were
driven from the whole of Bavaria, including the
neighboring Stadtamhof (1551).

The number of Jews expelled in 1519 is placed
at about 800; the number of their houses at 32.
While the population was probably smaller, it was

in any event not inconsiderable, namely, 5 to 10% of the total population, which was estimated at about 6000 to 8000. Fantastic records of the time picture the Jewish dwellings as imposing and magnificent edifices, and a contemporary ecclesiastical chronicler reports that Jews had in their possession portions of the Sinaitic Tablets of Moses and had carried them with them at the time of their departure. A number of the expelled Jews migrated to the southern Tyrol and to Italy with letters of safe-conduct provided by the Innsbruck administration.[184]

In the period of its "freedom from Jews", sessions of the Reichstag were held in Regensburg in 1532 and 1548, at which Josel of Rosheim appeared as the representative of Jewish interests. Josel was also active in endeavors to bring about an amelioration of conditions at the time of the Bavarian expulsion in 1551. He devoted himself to effecting the release of several Jews who were imprisoned in Munich and provided evidence on behalf of Jews by furnishing notarial attestation of old Privileges accorded them. The Jews had also turned for help to another outstanding contemporary, Martin Luther.

In their endeavor to obtain, if not the right of domicile, at least the right to occasional visits in the city of Regensburg, the Jews based their contention upon the rights of escort belonging to the hereditary marshals of the Empire, the Counts Pappenheim, which included the protection of the Jews. In the beginning the city authorities denied

in principle the right of entrance on passports
issued by the counts,[185] and in 1532 they placed
under arrest all Jews who presented these credentials.
In 1541, however, they found themselves constrained to acknowledge the validity of the
Pappenheim passports. Inasmuch as other cities,
which had likewise endeavored to keep the Jews
out of their territory, had denied the right of
escort of the Pappenheims, the Imperial Councilor
in 1580 established its validity. This precipitated a
peculiar situation in Regensburg when, in 1564, the
sessions of the Reichstag were permanently instituted there. The technical questions covered in these
deliberations also belonged to the province of the
hereditary marshals, who had no reason to oppose
the mercantile interests which the Jews were able
to obtain through the instrumentality of the
delegates of the princes in the Parliament. It is
reported, in this connection, that the delegation
from Saxony in particular had brought many Jews
with it to Regensburg.[186] A concession made to
the city provided that the Jews be lodged in an
outlying district and be required to have special
permits to leave it by day or night.[187] The contentions between the city and the hereditary
marshals continued uninterruptedly until the time
of the Emancipation period. In 1695 an enactment
promulgated by the hereditary marshal restricted
the number of Jews entitled to domicile in
Regensburg to four households. Residents exceeding
this quota were required to leave the city at the
expiration of three months; no lodging was to be

given to Jews from other localities; Jews were not
to be permitted to leave their dwellings on holidays
or at nights without special permission; they were
required to display yellow discs on their garments
as distinguishing symbols; carry on no profession
or trade; build no synagogue or *sukkah*, and reside
in quarters, if not remote, at any rate apart from
other dwellings. The restriction to four households
subsequently precipitated considerable discussion,
inasmuch as the Jews placed a wider construction
upon the rights accorded them by the terms of this
enactment than that intended by the municipal
authorities. To the discussions arising out of this
contention we are indebted for the preservation of
many reports on the subject of Jewish population.
Jews are reported resident in Regensburg as follows:

1694:—70 individuals; 1695:—4 families; 1698:—8
families; 1699:—10 families; 1715:—4 families;
1747:—7 families; 1777:—86 individuals; 1783:—88
individuals, of whom 42 were evicted; about
1800:—24 families (comprising about 110 individuals); 1810:—18 families; 1861:—about 150 families;
1871:—about 430 individuals; from that time until
the present day, about 150 families.

We recognize in these census reports the success
that attended the city's efforts to restrict the
number of its Jews. Among others, there were
evicted, in 1743, 42 individuals, most of whom
settled in smaller neighboring towns, such as
Kumpfmühl and Karthaus.[188] Resistance to Jewish
incursions on the part of the city was especially
violent about 1700, when the municipality

demanded the expulsion of all its Jews. Finally an appeal was taken to the Elector of Saxony as imperial Grand Marshal. The appeal was denied, the Elector fixing the number of Jews permitted residence in the city at six families. A characteristic phase is represented by the rapid increase up to 1861, and the subsequent complete cessation. Whereas other cities, as, for example, Munich and Augsburg, had experienced substantial increases of their Jewish populations up to 1900, a complete standstill ensued in Regensburg. The general development of the city, too, was retarded in comparison with that of other cities.

Significance also attaches to the selection of the Jews accorded the right of domicile. There were, in 1712, included in the small number of Jewish families, three Wertheimer families, relatives of the Vienna Court Factor, Samson Wertheimer, to whom the Elector of Saxony, on July 3, 1711, had awarded rights of domicile in Regensburg, which had been vacated by the deaths of authorized residents. Such domiciliary authorizations were manifestly obtainable only by influential Jews, such as, in 1692, Mayer Moses Wasserman, who had in that year, owing to the distress brought about by the French invasion, fled from the Rhineland; in 1712, Isaac Brodi; in 1715, Elkan Wasserman. It was especially the wealthy Jews, those subject to princes and embassies, and not those subject to the municipality, that the latter held in greatest fear. In the same manner as the city had appealed to the Elector of Saxony against the action taken by the Counts Pappenheim, it lodged in 1713 a protest against the former before the Imperial Assembly, which, however, referred its appeal back to the Counts. In 1721 and 1728 the city even protested directly to the Emperor and was able to point to the fact that it had, since 1519, uninterruptedly transmitted the medieval Jewish taxes to Austria, in consideration of being allowed to keep the city free of Jews. In 1737 the city's Bailiff sold his house on condition that it should not be leased to a Jew. Even on the threshold of the Emancipation period, 1780, there revived in the populace the memory of the ritual-murder legend: a Christian maidservant accused herself of having offered to sell a child to the Jew Lämlein. She was punished and compelled to leave the city. The period of "Enlightenment" had found other motives, not quite so crude, for the uninterruptedly continued Jewish hatred. In 1754 the *Regensburger Nachrichten* published violent attacks against the *Selihot* Prayers, basing their charges upon a publication by Chr. Wilhelm Christlieb, a converted Jew, entitled *Kurzer Auszug aus den Selichoth* (Brief Extracts from the *Selihot*).

Light is thrown upon the economic existence of the Jews in the years 1714 and 1733 by the enactment of new Jewish regulations. In these it is stated that they "are not permitted to conduct an open business place, shop or market stand," and therefore "their principal business practice and

income consists of lending money on pledges".[189]
There does not appear to have been any vestige in
Regensburg of the low moral standard of Jewish
business so frequently reported elsewhere in the
18th century. In 1803 the Hartleben newspaper
Fama published a warrant of arrest against a Jew,
Gabriel of Regensburg, on the charge of having,
together with several French Jews, forged official
documents. After the end of the 18th century there
are evidences of a resumption of Jewish participation in trade. All the Jews of Regensburg were then
engaged in the textile trade; Löw Mayer and the
widow Gumperz traded in coffee and sugar; Wolf
Henle and Philipp Reichenberger dealt in exchange,
the latter being also engaged in the wine business.

In 1803, following the Napoleonic territorial
changes, the city of Regensburg came under the
rule of the Elector of Mayence, Prince-Primate
Dalberg, who acquired from the Counts Pappenheim
the right to protect the Jews in consideration of a
flat payment of 1000 ducats (5400 fl.) and an
annuity of 1000 fl. The Counts had estimated the
yearly Jewish revenues at 9000 fl. and had asked
the sum of 32,000 fl. for this redemption. The
political independence of the city came to an end
with the advent of the Dalberg rule, and admission
or exclusion of the Jews was thenceforth subject to
the discretion of the new ruling power. In 1804
the Jewish body-tax was abolished.[190] The Jew,
Wolf Breidenbach of Offenbach, who had been

actively identified with bringing about this tax
annulment, made a personal visit to Regensburg at
this time. Feitel Katz of Regensburg, later known
as Philipp Reichenberger, gave his support to
Breidenbach in this matter.

As was the case elsewhere, the Jews of Regensburg
directed their efforts toward obtaining the rights
of unrestricted domicile and business independence.
They encountered in these efforts, as before, the
opposition of the Christian citizenry which lodged,
in 1807, a written protest with the government.
In consequence of the efforts of the two parties, the
Elector requested the Council of the realm to
submit an opinion (1809). Accordingly it was
enacted that unrestricted citizenship rights with
the privilege of wholesale trading be vested in
three families, namely, Philipp Reichenberger, Wolf
Henle and Philipp Seckel Wertheimer. Admission
was to be granted to such other Jewish families
only as were in possession of at least 2000 fl., and
these were to be accorded only the lesser rights of
citizenship (*Kleines Bürgerrecht*) upon annual payments of 50 fl. Their trading was to be restricted
to peddling, second hand goods, jewelry, precious
stones, old clothes and money-changing. The
purchase of land was to be permitted them only
when the transaction was effected in the name of
a Christian.

Philipp Reichenberger alone achieved prominence
as a man of great wealth and social importance.
He was Court Factor to the Princes of Thurn and
Taxis, to the Crown of Brandenburg-Ansbach, and

served as Fiscal Agent to the Crown of Prussia. He purchased in 1804 one of the most beautiful residences in the city, the former Dornberg Palace.

A curious circumstance is revealed in the appointment, about 1796, of Elias Gumperz as director of the Regensburg Theater. This post was acquired by him in consequence of money advanced by him against the box office receipts of the theater. It is reported that he met "with unanimous public approval" in his management of this playhouse, and that his activities were marked by "great efficiency, prompt payments and without any interference". It is to be borne in mind in this connection that the former Thurn and Taxis Theater, endowed with unlimited capital, had not been forgotten, and that it must be regarded as an achievement of no small moment that a Jewish money-lender of restricted means was able to carry on the local playhouse tradition without financial disaster, as had been the case with his predecessor.[191]

In 1810, Regensburg, by Napoleonic decree, was made subject to the Bavarian Crown, from which time the Jews of Regensburg participated in the general destiny of the Jews of Bavaria. Principally identified with the struggle for Jewish emancipation were, indeed, the larger Bavarian Jewish communities, Munich, Augsburg, Nuremberg, Bamberg, Fürth, Würzburg, although at times there was a participation in this movement by the small Regensburg community. The latter was a signatory to the appeal, in 1850, for the consummation of the Emancipation movement, and in 1860 the

community of Bamberg sought its coöperation in
annulling the law requiring the registration of Jews.
As late as the middle of the century the Regensburg
Jews were subjected to pressure at the hands of the
inimical Christian citizenry. For attendance at
the Regensburg Fair they were required to secure
a special certificate of good reputation from the
authorities.[192]

About the year 1800 religious services were still
being held in a Hall seating about 35 men and 28
women. It was located in the lane *"Hinter der
Grieb"*. The existence of this Hall was quietly
tolerated. The Jews, however, possessed no burial
ground of their own until 1822 and were compelled
to convey their dead to the Pappenheim or Fürth
cemeteries for interment. In the former, the Counts
Pappenheim exacted fees for the issuing of burial
permits. It was not until 1822 that a Jewish burial
ground was established in Regensburg, enlargements
being made in 1828 and 1869. A Jewish public
school was opened in 1832. In 1839–41 a synagogue
was built in the lower *Bachgasse* on the site of an
old patrician residence (Steyrerhaus), in existence
since the 14th century. A *Hebrah Kadishah* was
founded in 1863. Plans for the erection of a new
and larger synagogue were abandoned in 1867 on
account of the large outlay involved. It was not
until 1912 that the new and urgently needed
synagogue was dedicated.

CHAPTER VII

COMMUNAL DEVELOPMENTS

B. AUGSBURG

INFORMATION to the effect that Jews had already settled in Augsburg in the first century is gleaned from the writings of the scholarly Martin Welser of Augsburg (1594). There is no verification of this assertion and it is probably unverifiable. That an established Jewish community existed in Augsburg at the time of Emperor Frederick I (1152–90), can be accepted with certainty. It was this Emperor who interested himself in the restoration of the Jewry-regality and it would be surprising if there had been no Jews residing in his time in the city, which held the rank of an imperial residence. The earliest definite record has reference to a Jew, Josef of Augsburg, who is mentioned as a witness, in 1212.[193] It may be that the oldest tombstone in Augsburg (1231), which bears the name of Josef, marks his grave. The grounds for the indictment which appears to have been brought against Augsburg and all of Swabia by Rabbi Judah he-Hasid, are entirely unknown. He is supposed to have declared that no Rabbi resided in Augsburg, no *Kohen* (descendant of the priestly family of Aaron), no Jewish married couple, no one bearing the name of Eliezer, and that Swabia could produce no talmudical scholar.[194] Is it possible that this pronouncement bears reference to conditions of an Augsburg Jewry of which there exists no historic record?

It appears that the tribunal convoked in 1235 by Emperor Frederick II, growing out of the ritual-murder charge in Fulda, was held in Augsburg.[195]

In 1240–41 a calamity, of which no details are known, befell the Jews of Augsburg. This is revealed in an entry in the tax record which explains a tax deficiency as being due to a conflagration in which the taxpayers had perished.[196] The annual tax payments by the Jews at that time appear to have amounted to 20 lbs. This record would indicate the existence in Augsburg of an already established Jewish settlement.[197]

The question of Jewish taxation and Jewish control provoked at this time, in Augsburg also, a conflict between the city, the Bishop and the King. In 1247 contentions in these matters arose between the city and King Conradin. The influence of the Bishop was for the time being made secure through the episcopal ownership of the "Jewish House," i. e. the house of Jewish assembly. Its hypothecation to one of the citizens (1259) bears evidence of the encroaching demands made by the city.[198] In the 60's and 70's the latter was victorious in the rivalry for Jewish control. In the year 1266 the Bishop, as head of the municipality, requested King Conradin to act as his representative with the condition that he should not demand the return of revenues from Christians and Jews of which the Bishop had formerly been the recipient. The

Bishop had since that time been forced to relinquish
his control of Jewish affairs and his authority was
taken over by the city. On November 30, 1266, a
royal decree granted the city far-reaching rights
over its Jews.[199] The Jews were to make a single
payment of 70 lbs. to the King, covering a period
of five years, and to be relieved of any further
obligations. Admission of Jewish newcomers should
be arranged by two citizens in conjunction with
the Jews David and Liebmann. The protection
of the Jews should be turned over conjointly to two
prefects, one to be appointed by the King and one
by the city. By this action the city became to all
practical purposes invested with control of the
Jewish community. Upon the death of the King
shortly thereafter, the Bishop again entered the
ranks against the city's authority, even achieving
a temporary victory, as the city was no longer
enabled to invoke the royal support against him.
In the ensuing two years, responsibility for the
protection of the Jews was vested jointly in the
prefect of the Bishop and in the city. It was agreed
that the latter pay the Bishop an annual sum of
10 lbs., the Jews, however, to be relieved of any
direct payment to the Bishop. The controlling
influence of the city was thus maintained. The
municipal and the Jewry law, not the ecclesiastical
law, was to be invoked in cases of corpses thrown
into Jewish homes. It was a period when throughout Germany, ritual murder charges began to be
brought in ever larger numbers. That the city felt
itself secure in its control of Jewish protection is

evidenced in the codification of the municipal laws
of 1276. The municipal law regulated, before all
else, the economic relations between the Jews and
the Christian citizenry with special regard to the
conduct of the money-lending business. The Jews
were legally required to advance up to ⅔ of their
value upon proffered pledges of goods. This would
indicate that the Jews were already at that time
engaged in a well-developed credit business and that
this was regarded as an important factor in the
life of the Augsburg population. The Augsburg
municipal law served as a model, and numerous
other cities, Munich among them, adopted its
provisions. The independent status of the Jewish
community, despite the detailed regulations of the
municipal law, was much greater than it was at
the later period which is better known to us, inasmuch as the Jewish tribunal of that time still had
an extended criminal jurisdiction. It was empowered
to impose punishments, such as eye gouging, mutila-
tion of limbs, drowning and other extreme corporal
punishments, and to call upon the city for assistance in the execution of these sentences.[200]

The city went further still in its concern with
Jewish juridical interests. Following the example
set by Würzburg, it established in 1285 a new Jewish oath.[201] In 1290 it directed the establishing of
a new bathhouse for the special use of the Jews.
This was located on the lower estuary of the Lech,
the site at a later time of the *Spitalmühle*. This
bathhouse was named the *Rappenbad*.[202] The suggested derivation of this designation from the word

"Rabbi" is absurd. The new formula for the Jewish oath and the establishing of a bathhouse for the special use of Jews are to be regarded as measures directed to keeping the Jews separate from their Christian neighbors.

This restrictive municipal Jewish policy did not prevent the city, in periods of distress, from furnishing protection to the Jews against attacks upon their lives and property, on a compensatory basis. When, in 1298, they protected the Jews against the Rindfleisch attacks, the Jews had to pledge themselves to construct the so-called Jewish bastion, an extension of the city's fortifications. This bastion was in existence until 1704 when, in the war of the Spanish Succession, it was destroyed by the French. To secure the city's claims upon them the Jews were compelled to turn over as pledges to the municipality the synagogue and all their valuables. In 1308 they were again required to pay a sum of 500 lbs. to the city in consideration of protection accorded them in a time of peril.[203]

The above-mentioned Jewish bastion was a section of the city's fortifications that lay between the town moat and the Church of the Holy Cross. It was located near the Jewish burial ground in the vicinity of the present *Katzenstadel*, the burial ground being used until the time of the Jewish expulsion in 1438. The report that interments were continued to be made there until 1445 is hardly to be credited. The houses of the Jews were adjacent to the Bishop's Palace—an indication of the former relations of dependence upon the Bishop—in

the south-lying business center near the *Judenberg*,
and included the northern side of the present day
Weisse Gasse (White Street), the western side of the
Pfladergasse, the southern side of the Elias Holl Place
and the eastern side of the lower Hunold Moat.[204]

The business activities of the Jews, as revealed
by the municipal enactments of 1276, had at this
time already assumed the one-sided feature of
money-lending. That a period of commercial trading by the Jews of Augsburg preceded this later
restriction to credit business, as was the case in
Regensburg, is not proven. It may, however, have
been the case, as the general economic conditions
were the same as those in Regensburg. As early
as 1297 an Augsburg Jew appears as a creditor of
the Bavarian Dukes. At the beginning of the 14th
century,[205] Augsburg Jews actually acted as Court
bankers for the Dukes of Munich, and it was from
the latter that the Augsburg Jews Lamb and
Jüdlein received in 1304, in consideration of a debt
to them of 3600 fl., a lien against the Munich tax
receipts for a period of six years. In 1307 they
acknowledged to the city of Munich the receipt
of 750 fl.[206] On the whole the situation in Augsburg
presents the same picture as that given in our
description of the Regensburg Jewry. The city
was in need of credits for its manifold military and
political activities in a time of wars and individual
political aspirations. As we have seen above, the
records of Augsburg also fail to differentiate between
voluntary credit business, compulsory loans exacted
from the Jews, special tax levies in individual cases

and payments for protection accorded by the city
on special occasions. Only in isolated cases is the
origin of debt transactions discernible. The regular
Jewish taxes, payment of which was guaranteed
by the Jewry as a whole, are reported to have
amounted to 300 fl. in 1329. Special imposts were
laid upon the wealthy Jews; thus, for instance, in
1327–29, the Jewess Sprinzin was assessed in the
sum of 190 lbs., Isaac and Jacob 210 lbs. In 1321
the city levied an assessment of 1200 fl. upon the
Jews, the reason for which is not known, and in
1329, again exacted a loan from Lamb. In 1346,
the Jews paid a ground rent of 247 lbs. on their
Town House, the garden adjacent to their burial
place, and on several dwelling houses. In addition
a rental obligation of 12½ lbs. was placed upon
"the little house of Ganser", and not less than 330
lbs. was levied upon the house of the "wealthy
Karpflin".[207] Despite unquestionably heavy money
payments by the Jews, the needs of the city were of
so pressing a nature that a compulsory loan was also
exacted from the Christian citizenry. The Bishop,
too, was heavily indebted to the Jews at this time.[208]

The relation in which the Jews stood to the
Bavarian dukes, formerly a simple relation of
debtor and creditor, changed temporarily when,
in 1314, one of the dukes of Munich ascended the
German throne. The proximity and the economic
importance of Augsburg induced King Louis, who
was involved in numerous costly political entanglements, to take an energetic attitude in the matter
of tax levies, especially upon the Jews. It was he

who originated the "gold penny offering", that
Jewish head tax which long outlived all the
Medieval Jewish communities. His proximity and
his power brought about a temporary transference
of the city's control of its Jewry. He hypothecated
the Augsburg Jewish taxes among creditors and
favorites.[209] The interest of the city in the protection of the Jews was lessened in the same degree
that the Jewish body became an enclave of royal
interests within the confines of the city walls.
Another circumstance, too, threatened the situation
in which the Jews found themselves. Since the
20's, economic depressions, mounting costs of living,
and the large municipal indebtedness had made it
impossible for the city even to meet the interest
on its own obligations or to redeem them upon
maturity. The Emperor took advantage of this
desperate situation again to draw the Jewish control
to himself, indemnifying the city, however, by
forcing the Jews on pain of imprisonment to deliver
to the city their bonds of indebtedness.[210] The
wealthiest of the Jews at that time appear to have
been Jacob, the son of Lamb; Sprinzin, wife of the
Schoolmaster; Ernstlin Ganser and Josef Kratzer.

The reign of King Louis brought to the fore in
the meantime another rival for the Jewish control,
namely the Bishop, whose claims were revived by
the condition of the times, as King Louis, who died
suddenly in 1347, had stood under ecclesiastical
excommunication. For this reason the pretensions
of the Bishop received the support of the late King's
opponent, who subsequently became Charles IV

(1347–76) and who enjoyed the Papal favor. He
released the Bishop in 1348 from all indebtedness
to the Jews and invested him with control over a
group of specifically designated Jews. This control
was of a special nature and independent of the
former municipal, and now again royal dominion.[211]
In association with the subsequently restored municipal Jewish control, this episcopal domination
was continued through many generations. In 1350
the King renewed the Bishop's authority to "look
after the Jews" (*Juden zu heimen*).[212]

Added to these economic and political circumstances, which had brought about the city's loss
of interest in the Jews, was the fact that the Burgomaster at that time, a man heavily indebted to
the Jews, was a spendthrift and an unscrupulous
politician. He was a scion of the Regensburg
patrician family, Portner, members of which played
a deplorable rôle in the later history of the Jews
of Regensburg. It is said of him that he opened
the city gate to the "Jew Killers" (*Judenschläger*)
in 1349 and thereby precipitated the annihilation
of the Jewish community.

The King and the city divided the property of
the massacred Jews, and the former commissioned
the city to liquidate the Jewish property, permitting
the municipality to cancel its own indebtedness to
the Jews, and claiming for himself only so much of
this property as remained. Duke Frederick of
Teck, in his capacity as governor, was charged with
the function of realizing on the property (May 30).
At the same time the Emperor relieved the city of

responsibility in connection with the massacre of
the Jews. In 1355 he again granted the city—as
he had to the Bishop in 1350—the right to give
domicile to Jews, including the right to levy taxes
upon them for a period of twelve years.[213] In 1359,
he extended this term for an additional twenty
years.[214] The municipality, however, was not
granted the powers which it desired and which it
had formerly possessed, namely the unrestricted
control of Jewish affairs in its territory, as its Jewish jurisdiction was withheld, being placed in the
hands of the imperial prefect, evidently at the
request of the Jews. The desire of the city for the
resumption of the former complete dominion of its
Jewry is evidenced in the fact that it had in 1364,
with the concurrence of the Emperor, obtained for
itself, upon payment of 500 lbs., the lien on the
Jewish taxes (formerly held by Hoheneck) which
had been established in the days of King Louis.[215]

The city was all the more determined to hold
fast to its diminished control of the Jews, and for
this reason prevented, as was the case in other cities,
their departure from the city. In 1356, Zeruyah
was compelled to make oath that he would remain
in the city until the expiration of the term granted
for Jewish domicile by the Emperor (the 12 years
of the authorization of 1355).[216]

The disturbed condition of the times appears to
have had a deleterious effect upon the Jews themselves. In the municipal register of those punished
for serious crimes there is an increase at this time in
the number of Jewish offenders. It is not likely that

the Kufsteiner who was charged with looting at the
time of the Jewish massacres (1348) and subsequently punished, was a Jew.[217] The same is probably true in the case of "Sophie, the Jewess" who
was punished in 1349 as a thief, an adulteress and a
wicked person (*Böse Haut*). Here, too, the un-Jew-
ish name might seem strange, but it was precisely in
Augsburg that it is reported in the year 1384 that
the Jew Hartmann (Ezekiel)—doubtless following
upon conviction by the court—was punished by the
Rabbinate with banishment from the city.[218] There
are reports of outrages committed in 1372 by the
Jews Mosse and Mathys, and of the lewd practices
of a vagabond Jew (*Schalantjude*); and, in 1382,
of the habitual drunkenness of a Jew, who received
a sentence of five years' banishment from the city.
Two attempts at extortion from Jews are finally
mentioned, the bases of which were alleged seduc-
tion of Christian married women. These reports
of demoralization of the Augsburg Jews at the time
of the Black Death are to be viewed in the light
of the general moral breakdown of that period.
The general demoralization is clearly evidenced in
the pages of the Augsburg register of persons
punished for serious crimes from which the foregoing instances are culled. Not until the downfall
of the government in 1368 was there an improvement in the character of the police administration,[219]
and such widespread criminal activities are not
found among the Jews in later times.

The instability of general living conditions,
especially among the Jews, is indicated by mani-

festations of unrest in the public as well as in the
Jewish life of that time. There was an uprising of
the guilds against the ruling families in 1368, and
in 1372 there followed a war with the Bavarian
dukes. In 1380, there was a severe epidemic (*ein
grosser Sterb*). The economic existence of this period
was also subjected to great disturbances, and after
the great depopulation caused by the pestilence of
1348–49 there arose many changes in the economic
order. In the case of the Augsburg Jews, it was
enacted in 1378 that Jewish claims upon the estates of
deceased debtors be legally registered,[220] a requirement
that indicates progress in economic development.

Evidence of the extent to which the Jews were
affected by the prevailing unrest is provided by
the repeated coming and going of wealthy Jews.
Michael of Ulm was a Jewish citizen in Augsburg
in 1384. He left the city at that time but returned
again in 1396. Duke Stephen of Bavaria registered
a request with the city of Augsburg that it refuse
domicile to his Jew Sanwel, so that the Duke might
not come into bad repute (*Unglimpf*) on account
of the imposition of exorbitant taxes he had made
upon him. In 1382 the Jew Bendit of Munich was
granted domicile in Augsburg. The records of the
city of Regensburg, as we have seen, afford similar
instances of frequent changes of Jewish residence
in this period. That we have fewer records of such
migration in Augsburg is probably due to the
political disturbances in this city, which ended only
after a recognition of the guilds as factors in the
city's administrative affairs.

The city's authority in its relation to the Jewish community did not remain unchallenged. Recognition of its rights by the Kings cost money, and every change of government brought complicated negotiations with it. These negotiations proved especially disadvantageous to the Jews in the reigns of the Luxemburg Kings, Charles IV and Wenceslaus. They were held under arrest in 1374 until they had furnished a sum of 10,000 fl. demanded by the King, a demand which the city had made futile efforts to resist on their behalf. In 1381, the Jews were again cast into prison pending payment by them of 5000 fl. demanded by the city for its requirements in a military campaign. Finally, following an additional demand for 22,000 fl. in 1384, the Jews were again placed under arrest.

The city endeavored without avail to protect the Jews from demands made upon them by King Wenceslaus in 1385. After protracted negotiations an agreement was finally reached by which the Swabian cities, including Augsburg, were to remit to the Emperor the sum of 40,000 fl., and they, on their part, to requite themselves, to the best of their ability, with assessments upon the Jews. The extent to which the city of Augsburg was mulcted in this assessment of 40,000 fl. is not known, nor is it revealed in the records how much the city received through the annulment of its indebtedness to the Jews.

At the time of the second Jewish debt cancellation (1390), the city of Augsburg again endeavored to offer resistance , as was the case in other cities.

The need of solidarity among the confederated municipalities in resisting the demands made upon them by the King was so great that the neighboring city of Nördlingen, which had, in 1384, at the time of dissensions about the Jews, countenanced massacres and looting in its Jewish quarter, was excluded from the confederation with the support of Augsburg and Regensburg. After the military defeat of the cities (1388), their position in relation to the royal demands became less secure. The King brought every one of them to compliance with his will. In the case of Augsburg, too, he was compelled to resort to coercion. He imprisoned Augsburg merchants returning from the Frankfort Fair, and by this means enforced the payment of 1800 gulden by the city, the latter receiving, in requital, permission from the King to retain its Jews for a further period of 12 years and to have the entire benefit of all imposts upon them without a renewal of any demands upon them on the part of the King. The city was compelled to borrow the sum of 1800 fl. That they did not borrow this money from the Jews, which would have been the natural procedure, can only be regarded as evidence of the fact that the Jews were no longer in a position to furnish such a sum. It is to be noted, however, that the loan was obtained from the King's own chamberlain, Borziwoy von Swynar, the confidential agent of the King in the matter of the Jewish debt cancellation, and that the city was compelled to pay him a usurious rate of interest.[221] The sum of 1800 fl. would appear to be a relatively small amount in view of the importance of the city. It may have represented only the payment in a final accounting, or had the ability of the Jews to raise such a sum been weakened to such an extent in 1392?

The scattered data concerning the Jewish population and the taxes to which they were subjected may properly be brought together at this place. The figures here given have only an approximate value, owing to the difficulties attending an accurate determination in the records of the Middle Ages.

Population:
    1355: about 18 families
    1356: 23 families
    1368: 40 families
    1382: 46 families
    1385: about 200 individuals
    1401: 17 tax-paying families

Tax Payments:
    1346: see above, p. 178.
    1350–62: none, or very insignificant.
    1363: only 82 pf. land property tax.
    Seelgerät (Foundation), valued at 180 lb., taxed at 5%.
    1363–80: Dance Hall, at an increasing tax of 3½s, 14s, 1 fl.
    1367: Jewish land property tax 3.32% (Christian 1.66%).
    1368: Jewish land property tax 4.98% (Christian 1.66%).
    1376: Jewish land property tax 3.32% (Christian 3.32%).[222]

It is revealed in the foregoing figures that: (1) there was a definite decline in the number of Jewish tax-paying residents, probably associated with the general decline in Jewish population, following upon the happenings of 1384, 1385 and 1390; (2) a definite increase in the amount of Jewish taxes in 1368, the year of political crisis; a doubling of the Christian land taxes during the war of the municipal confederation, together with a reduction of the Jewish taxes to the rate in effect before the revolution; in connection with which abatement it must of course be borne in mind that the special assessments to which the Jews were subjected off-set any apparent advantage thus accorded them.

Following upon the deposing of the drink-sodden King Wenceslaus (1400), there came into existence, with the ascension of King Ruprecht, a royal over-lord of the Jews who was in a state of continual financial embarrassment and who used every means to increase his income from Jewish sources. As early as August 16, 1401, he renewed for a period of 10 years the right of the city to grant domicile to the Jews, with the old established provision that half of the Jewish taxes and the "golden penny offering" be reserved for the King.[223] The city, too, it appears, following the security inherent in this authorization, began once more to consider methods of securing revenue from the Jews. The municipality again invited Jews to become residents, thus, in 1406, Abraham of Eichstätt was granted domicile upon payment of an admission fee of 12 fl. and an annual tax of 4 fl.; in 1409, the

Jewish "Meister" Koppelman was admitted on payment of 28 fl. and 12 fl. respectively, and his brother on payment of 24 fl. and 10 fl. In 1422 Lazarus of Wertingen was admitted upon payment of 15 fl. and 5 fl.

A Jewish policy expressly based upon financial considerations was also adopted by Ruprecht's successor to the throne, King Sigmund (1411–37). He immediately demanded from the city half of the income from the Jewish taxes and the "gold penny offering".[224] The former amounted at that time to 200 fl. annually and was payable on Martinmas (November 11). A methodical collection of the "gold penny offering" in Augsburg or elsewhere is not conceivable, inasmuch as its prerequisite, a reliable census of the Jewish population, was not available. It was not difficult, therefore, to reach an agreement, when the city, in 1415, in consideration of the above-mentioned Privilege of 1411, resisted compliance with the demand for payment of the "gold penny offering". The compromise was based upon the payment of a lump sum of 200 fl., which included the estimated returns from the "gold penny offerings". A definite clarification of the "gold penny offering" liability in favor of the King was avoided in the Augsburg as well as in the related Regensburg negotiations. Following the agreement reached in 1415, the Privilege accorded the city was extended to an additional term of twelve years; the King in this connection giving assurance that future hypothecations of the Jews to third persons be null and void.[225] In the mean-

time, the collection of the "gold penny offerings"
in Augsburg was delegated in 1417 to a Jewish
commissioner, in the name of the Emperor,[226] and
the city's fundamental opposition overruled. The
royal promise in the matter of future hypothecation referred apparently to Count Pappenheim,
who had in 1415 been entrusted with the collection
of the King's Jewish taxes. At a subsequent period,
1429, the Pappenheim claims were, however, again
brought to the fore.[227] The King accorded him one
half of the Jewish taxes and the "gold penny
offering", and the Jews pledged themselves to pay
him yearly a sum of 200 lbs. in satisfaction of these
claims. In 1422, the King commissioned the Count
Palatine John with the collection of the "gold
penny offering". The city resisted this action on
the basis of the Privilege of 1415. An agreement
was not reached until 1425, the Jews pledging themselves to pay 50,700 Bohemian *groschen* within a
period of 1¼ years. In 1431, the King again levied
an extraordinary impost upon the Jews, with the
promise, however, of a tax immunity for a period
of 12 years. There were at that time only nine
taxable Jews, whose combined payments amounted
to 1500 fl.[228] This promise did not, however,
prevent another tax demand by King Sigmund in
1434, a newly devised coronation tax, which was
subsequently levied by all the Emperors at the
time of their coronations. The coöperation of the
Jewish community in this matter was negotiated
by Meister Jacob Rabi (i. e. Jacob Weil?) and the
Jew Feyvelmann. The personal efforts of the great

Rabbi and the promise made by the Emperor at
the same time that no further extraordinary taxes
be demanded and that no cancellation of indebtedness be enacted against the Jews of Augsburg bear
evidence that the negotiations had been of a difficult
nature and that the King had made threats. It is
not known how much the Jews of Augsburg were
assessed in the new Papal Bull Tax (*Bullensteuer*)
created by King Sigmund on the basis of the efforts
of the Emperor in obtaining the Jewish Protection
Bull from Pope Martin V. It may be that no payments were made in this connection. The reason
is suggested in the complaint made by the King's
chamberlain, Conrad von Weinsberg, in 1417, that
the King's moiety of the Jewish taxes yielded only
43 fl. It seems therefore that the financial capacity
of the Jews was exhausted. The Privilege accorded
Feyvelmann, 1433–34, was evidently compensatory
for his support in the matter of the coronation tax
levy. The circumstances make it probable that he
was the wealthiest among the Jews and personally
shouldered a major portion of the tax.

Another circumstance pointing to the impoverished condition of the Jews and their diminished
taxable usefulness is revealed in the increasing
repressive measures again adopted toward them.
In 1434 the King, at the instance of the city,
directed a rigorous enforcement of the distinctive
Jewish garb. At the same time, the city prohibited
the free interment of alien Jews in the Jewish burial
ground. In 1436, the municipality ordered the
discontinuance of the Jewish juridical autonomy.[229]

Repressive measures reached a peak in 1438 with
the expulsion of the Jews, whose impoverished
condition had brought about this deplorable situation, although the actual causes are traceable to
the distress prevailing in the city. The records
reveal the appearance of devastating epidemics in
1420, 1430 and 1437. Even though there may be
an exaggeration in the reported mortality figures
of 16,000, or in some cases 6,000,[230] the reaction
upon the Jews was unavoidable, as these devastating plagues were supposed by the people of the
Middle Ages to fall within the sphere of religious
phenomena.

This situation was further aggravated by the
economic condition of the times. Speculation in
food stuffs, failure of crops and money devaluation
imperiled industry and precipitated an inadequate
food supply. From about 1415 to about 1435 there
was a fiscal devaluation of at least 50%. The price
of corn in 1417 was five times greater than it was,
for example, in 1420. Within a period of two weeks,
in 1433, there occurred an increase of fully 50%,
from 2 lbs. to 3 lbs. per bushel (*Schaff*). By 1437
the price had risen to five times this figure, as much
as 10 lbs. It was not until 1438–39 that it again fell
to 2 lbs., i. e. to the 1433 level.[231]

Added to the poverty of the Jews and the tense
economic and unsanitary conditions, there was the
strained religious situation evoked in the period
of the Ecclesiastical Councils (the Council of
Constance, 1414–18, and the Council of Basle,
1431–49) and the religious wars (War of the Huss-

ites, 1419–1436). The condition of the Jews was imperiled from every quarter.

If there existed any connection between the Jewish expulsion of 1438 and the immediately following decline in the price of corn, which the lack of preliminary investigations renders uncertain, the connection cannot be charged to an independent speculation in food stuffs on the part of the Jews, for there is not the slightest evidence of such speculation by them. Nor is there any likelihood, in view of the small number of Jews in the city, that their departure as consumers could have had any effect upon the fall in prices. The Jewish expulsion in itself, as an economic-political phenomenon, could not, therefore, be justified by these circumstances. In the light of the tense situation the expulsion was not at all necessary, as the departure of the Jews was a voluntary consequence of the prevailing distress. There were in the city in 1437 only 27 tax-paying Jews in contrast with 32 in the year 1428, and 9 in 1431, clearly indicating large haphazard fluctuations. In 1438, before the time of the expulsion, mention is made in the municipal tax records of the departure of eight Jewish families. On July 7, 1438, the Jews were ordered to evacuate the city by St. Kilian (July 8), 1439. The number of Jews at that time is given as 300. It appears that even as late as 1440 there were some Jews remaining, as in this year the Jews were again ordered by the municipal authorities to dispose of their houses and to remove from the city within two years. It is possible that an extension of time had been granted the wealthier Jews, as was the case in many other cities. Report to the effect that as late as 1445 Jewish burials were still made in the Augsburg cemetery would, if they occurred at all, be more reasonably explainable on this ground. As early as 1439 no mention is made of Jewish taxes in the municipal tax records.[232] After the departure of the Jews, their Dance Hall was converted into a mill, the bathhouse disposed of, the site of the burial ground included in the development of the city's fortifications (1523), and the tombstones used in large measure for reconstruction work in the Town Hall.

The duty devolved upon the city to come to an understanding with persons having claims upon the Jews. The assent of King Albrecht had already been secured by the city. As this assent, however, was not given in writing, King Frederick III, the successor of Albrecht, to whose attention the absence of this formality had been drawn by an enemy of the city, protested in 1456 against the Jewish expulsion. He had been informed that a buried treasure in the Ghetto had been taken over by the city authorities. Accordingly he absolved the latter of responsibility in the matter, in consideration of the payment by them of 13,000 fl., and granted them the privilege of taking in and expelling Jews at their discretion.[233]

The Counts Pappenheim also still retained their right to the Jewish taxes, and the city was therefore constrained to reach an agreement with them also. These negotiations were continued until

Easter of 1441, being finally adjusted with the coöperation of the Bishop of Eichstätt by the payment by the city of 1400 fl. to the Counts, and the renunciation by the latter of their claims against the Jews.[234]

These transactions effected the complete destruction of the Jewish community within the city of Augsburg, although the Jews who came under episcopal protection remained unmolested for the time being. The homes of the latter—at any rate in any appreciable number—were not in the city proper, but in various sections of the Augsburg diocese, principally in Dillingen. Their number appears to have been insignificant.

Following their expulsion from the city, many of the Jews found domicile in its immediate vicinity, in part in episcopal domains such as Oberhausen, some in other places that did not lie within the jurisdiction of the city, although included in the sphere of its economic activities. The principal among these Jewish settlements from the 16th century on, namely Kriegshaber, Steppach and Pfersee, achieved important significance.

In the centuries that followed, the efforts of the city were not so much directed to the expulsion of the Jews from its juridical influence as to a prevention of their participation in its economic affairs. These efforts, however, could not result in a victory wherever the Jews succeeded in securing the intervention of the rulers in opposition to the stand taken by the city. Detrimental to the purposes of the municipality was the close proximity of one of these neighbors, the Imperial House (the Margravate of Burgau) itself, whose dominion included the township of Pfersee, which was a possible source of permanent protective influence for the Jews. There is in fact a tradition of a later date that the wealthiest among the Jews selected Pfersee, among the environs of Augsburg, as their place of residence.

After the city had, with the expulsion of the Jews, relinquished its claim upon juridical and economic Jewish affairs, the episcopal influence in these matters was augmented. In the latter half of the 15th century the Bishop was frequently called upon by the citizens of Nördlingen to act as arbiter in disputes relating to the exaction of Jewish usury. In 1479 the Nördlingen Jews were granted an extension of one year in their term of domicile upon the condition that their legal disputes with Christians be submitted for adjudication to the episcopal tribunal in Augsburg. The Jews again came into contact with the Augsburg municipal officialdom also. The memorial formulated in 1530 by the Swabian cities against the Jews and submitted to the Augsburg Diet appears to have been the work of Conrad Peutinger, the famous municipal scribe of Augsburg. Among the signatories to this memorial were the cities of Augsburg and Regensburg. In a dispute between the city and Count Oettingen in 1538 regarding Jewish affairs, the municipality was represented by one of its citizens, Dr. Bernhard Rehlinger. At the sessions of the Augsburg Diet in 1530 and 1548, Jewish economic matters were circumstantially discussed. In Augsburg, too, there

had been extended negotiations between the city
of Regensburg and King Maximilian (1516–18), with
the purpose of bringing about the expulsion of the
Jews from Regensburg.[235] When his successor to
the throne, King Charles V, raised a question as
to the harmful effects the driving out of the Jews
might have upon his interests, the Speyer Diet
(1523) was compelled to take up for consideration
the matter of Jewish revenues (*Judengeld*); and
Augsburg, too, participated in this discussion. The
citizens of Augsburg themselves also saw to it that
the Jews and their affairs should not fade from
memory. It was impossible to dissolve entirely
the commercial relations that existed between the
citizens and the neighboring Jews, as had been
contemplated by the city, and efforts were consequently directed toward rendering these relations
more difficult. It was ordered by the municipality
in 1536 that Jews be denied admission to the city
for purposes of trade, but should only be permitted
entrance when their appearance was required in
the adjusting of legal matters. This ruling was
reënacted in 1544. In 1538 the borrowing of money
from Jews was prohibited and it was found necessary to repeat this interdiction in 1541, 1545 and
1553. Failure to comply with this prohibition was
punished with the loss of citizenship. In 1540 it
was ordered that every Jew who made temporary
visits to the city be placed in charge of a personal
escort (*lebendiges Geleit*) and that the duration of
such visits be limited to one day. In 1546, it was
further decided that Jews be permitted to have

entrance to the city only when such visits were of
benefit or advantage to the municipality. In 1540
the citizens were forbidden to give lodgement or
shelter to Jews. The latter were compelled to reim-
burse the city for the cost of the personal guards
assigned them. This payment was fixed at the
rate of 20 kr. per diem.[236]

From the continued repetition of these identical
prohibitory enactments it becomes evident that a
number of the citizens were not in entire sympathy
with the city's restrictive policy. Pfersee belonged
at that time to an Augsburg citizen named Sailer.
He thwarted the policy of the municipality by
permitting the Jews to remain in this town. In
1559, the municipality took steps in an appeal to
the Archduke Ferdinand to have the Jews expelled
from Pfersee. This attempt proved futile. The
number of Jews who were settled in the suburbs
of Augsburg at that time is not known. That there
were altogether only five Jews in these townships
in 1571 is hardly believable.[237]

The transference of Jewish domicile from the
city of Augsburg to its suburbs did not affect the
character of the economic and social living conditions of the Jews. They continued to engage in
the business of money-lending and were subjected
to the same arraignments as before the expulsion.
They were accused, as before, of the murder of
Christian children and were again driven out of
several of the places in which they had sought
refuge.[238] In the episcopal township of Oberhausen,
a Christian maidservant is reported to have offered

to sell a child to the Jews (1560). The Bishop (in 1574) expelled the Jews from Oberhausen and in 1575 from all the districts within his jurisdiction. Preceding this expulsion, as was often the case elsewhere, there had been an intensified enforcement of the rule requiring Jews to wear a distinctive garb marked with yellow badges.[239] The business of the Jewish money-lenders in the vicinity of Augsburg is reported to have approximated, about the year 1570, a yearly sum of 60,000 to 80,000 fl., at an annual interest of 50%. The city's residents, it was complained, were mulcted in the sum of 36,000 fl. yearly through the Jews.[240] This accounting was undertaken for the purpose of considering the advisability of establishing a municipal money-lending organization. Such an organization was effected in 1573. It was incorporated with the Almonry, and was designed to make loans in the amounts of 2 to 10 fl. to indigent applicants at a low rate of interest. In the period of scarcity that ensued in 1591, the municipality created a fund of 30,000 fl. to be loaned at a 5% annual interest rate, and it is reported that loans had been made upon 1500 pledges within the period of a few months. It had taken fully 150 years before the authorities came to a realization of the fact that the operation of the Jewish money-lending business was required by the needs of its Christian population, and that the mere expulsion of the Jews certainly failed to bring about a satisfactory solution of this problem. The city sought to secure its Jewish exclusion policy, even in the face of the influence exerted by the King

as protector of the Jews, and obtained from Rudolf
II, in 1599, a confirmation of its prohibitory enactments relating to Jewish trading and money-lending.
It was not until 1601 that official publication of this
decree was made. As early as 1602 the publication
of this decree had to be renewed and penalties were
provided anew for failure to comply with its provisions. The transgressors were mulcted in the
amount of their overcharge, i. e. the overvaluation
of the pledges. To prevent evasions of the money-
lending interdiction, the transfer of Jewish pledges
to Christians was forbidden.

Interference with the carrying out of the municipal Jewish policy was injected from two quarters.
The Jews of Pfersee were subjects of the Habsburgs,
i. e. the imperial house, and were exempt from the
penalties provided by the above-mentioned municipal decree of 1602. A rigorous application to
them of the municipal policy of repression would
have provoked the opposition of the King. The
other interference with the operation of the municipal Jewish policy was caused by the wars that were
waged throughout Germany, almost without inter-
ruption, since 1618. Time and again, the city of
Augsburg was compelled to grant admission to the
neighboring Jews to protect them from military
attacks. But as soon as the emergency had passed,
it took immediate steps to drive them out. In
consideration of the protection thus accorded them,
payments were exacted from the Jews, who were
also frequently subjected to compulsory loans.
In 1632 the Jews of Pfersee appealed to the Arch-

duke Ferdinand to obtain for them permission
from the city authorities to seek refuge in the city
of Augsburg from the approaching troops of the
King of Sweden. On this occasion the city denied
their request. In 1636, at the approach of the
imperial cuirassiers, the Jews of Pfersee were granted
temporary shelter (*Beisitz*) by the city of Augsburg,
but with the reservation that they should not trade
in precious metals. In 1639 the Jews of Pfersee,
who had again been admitted to Augsburg, were
required to pay the same quartering-tax (*Quartier-
anlage*) as that exacted from the citizens. In 1641
they were again accorded temporary quarters. It
was ordered in 1642 that the Jews quartered in the
city should not engage in trade and should not be
permitted to appear in the streets without personal
escort, an exception being made in the case of the
war-contractor Isaac Ulmann, who had been admitted to the city in 1641 by imperial direction.
The efforts made by the city again to drive out the
Jews were directed—in complete contrast to the
policy pursued in the Middle Ages—especially
against the rich among them, as it was feared they
would engage in money-lending activities. A secret
municipal decree of those days provided that the
poorer Jews who were unable to lend money be
treated more leniently in the matter of local
domicile.[241] The Jews were directed in 1645 to
turn over all the pledges held by them to the municipal pawnshop.

The city's antipathy to the wealthier Jews above
referred to could not, however, be permanently

realized in its practical policy. The uninterrupted
continuance of the war and the consequent money
requirements brought about a greater dependence
upon the coöperation of the richer and more capable
business administrators among the Jews. This is
implied in the above-noted exception made in the
case of Isaac Ulmann. The wealthy Jews enjoyed
not only the protection of the rulers whom they
served, and to whose wishes the city was frequently
compelled to yield, but they were in a position to
be useful to the city itself in many ways, through
their ability to provide financial aid. The citizens
were not oblivious to these conditions. The outstanding Augsburg merchant, Ferdinand von
Rehlingen, had as his representative in Lyons
a Jew by the name of Elias Nathan.[242] It was a
question of an economic-political nature whether
the danger to the citizens from Jewish business
activities outweighed the advantage accruing there-
from to the city finances or vice versa. The many
wars brought about a smouldering controversy
which continued for centuries between the merchants
and the municipal authorities regarding this problem.

In the year 1645, i. e. at about the time of the
termination of the Thirty Years' War, the city
extended the right of residence (*Beisitz*) to the Jews
who had taken refuge within its walls on condition
that they execute a compulsory loan of 5000 fl. at
an annual interest rate of 5%. In the same year
the Jews were compelled to make another loan of
1500 thalers to the city and were subjected in

addition to special taxes of various designations. These, too, were increased in 1545. As a matter of fact these loans were not repayable, inasmuch as the prevailing inflation made them worthless in a very short time. It is significant in this connection that the city in levying these extraordinary imposts upon the Jews completely reversed its former policy, as these levies naturally implied recognition of Jewish business activity. That the attitude taken by the city in these matters was one of reluctance is indicated by the fact that immediately following the conclusion of Peace (1648) it decided to banish all the Jews from the city, on the ground that their toleration within its territory was "contrary to old custom."[243] It was primarily the Protestant faction of the citizenry that manifested the most virulent opposition to the Jews.

The Thirty Years' War had greatly weakened the influence of the German citizenry for a long period. The diminution of its power lessened also its traditional authority in the regulation of Jewish affairs. In contrast to this decline of middle class influence, there had developed a greater power on the part of the princes and rulers, i. e. those who suffered no economic disadvantage from the toleration of the Jews, but might rather look forward to financial advantages. The city was compelled in the 17th and 18th centuries to subordinate itself to the continually growing influence exerted by the rulers.

If we have emphasized in the foregoing analysis the influence of economic interests upon the shaping

of the Jewish policy, coöperating factors of the
religious attitude and motives should not be overlooked. In the nature of the case these are not so
clearly recognizable, but they are found to have
existed among the citizens as well as among the
rulers. The intensive coöperation of the Protestant
citizenry in the renewed efforts to drive out the
Jews, following the Peace of 1648, affords evidence
of religious motives in this matter. These are also
clearly indicated in the attitude taken by the
Elector Max II of Munich. The strained relations
between the different Christian denominations led
to such petty discriminations that even their pig-
sties were separated from each other. These circumstances prevented the more recent attempts at
Jewish expulsion from Augsburg from being completely carried out. In 1680 the city again decreed
the banishment of the Jews and the closing of
their "stalls," i. e. their trading shops. It is thus
revealed that the Jews had not only permanent
residence in the city, but conducted business places.

The Jews living in Pfersee held a peculiar position as compared with the Jewish residents in the
other suburbs of Augsburg. This township belonged
in part to the Augsburg *Jakobspfründe* (St. James'
Benefice) and in part to the Margravate of Burgau,
a circumstance which brought about a different
treatment of its Jews from that obtaining in Kriegshaber and Steppach, where they were regarded as
strangers. The latter made efforts for this reason
to become subjects of the municipality through the
Jakobspfründe, as had the Jews of Pfersee. When

these efforts miscarried, they endeavored in 1721
to find homes in Oberhausen, which came under
the domination of the Martin Foundation of
Augsburg. The Jews of Pfersee, basing their claim
upon the indirect backing of the imperial authority,
asked to be permitted visits to the city in the
capacity of "Roman citizens", and were supported
in this contention by the Innsbruck administration.

Coincident with the variations in the rights of
Jews to visit the city, the assessments levied upon
Jews were subject to continual changes, the demands
made upon them fluctuating between exactions
from individuals and lump-sum indemnities from
the Jewish communities, in some cases single
families or business establishments. At the time of
the Swedish occupation in 1634, the assessment for
each person was 12 kreutzer for the morning and 6
kr. for the afternoon. In subsequent negotiations in
this matter an agreement was finally reached fixing
the daily payment at 30 kr., which included the
personal attendance costs. At times of scarcity
there was a temporary increase of 1 fl. in the assessment, with subsequent reduction to 30 kr.

The receipt of this income from the Jews did not
prevent the city from constantly thinking of their
expulsion, and it is, therefore, to be assumed that
the income from this source was not sufficiently
large. As a matter of fact, the records of the 18th
century give frequent indication that the personal
attendance charges remained unpaid. The city
possessed no powers of enforcing payment of these
delinquencies, as the greater number of the Jews

residing in the suburbs were under the jurisdiction
of other powers. In the Middle Ages the city had
exercised a widespread control over the Jews, as
these were subject to the jurisdiction of the Municipal Court. By its expulsion of the Jews the city
had lost this control. Besides, those Jews who were
favored by the powerful rulers by reason of their
wealth were also protected by these rulers in regard
to the taxes imposed by the city, whereas the poorer
Jews could provide only paltry returns. The city
sought to control the Jewish escort tax by limiting
the right of entrance of the Jews exclusively through
the Gögginger gate.

The difficult situation in which the city found
itself is revealed in the negotiations of the year
1719. A municipal councilor advised the city authorities that inasmuch as an absolute exclusion of Jews
was not practicable, they should be accorded free
admission to the city, so that the latter should not
be restricted to bearing the burden of their competitive business abilities the while others reaped the
advantage of receiving their taxes.[244] Others, too,
expressed themselves as favoring the admission of
the Jews, with the proviso that they advance a
loan to the city without charging interest. In the
meantime the expulsion idea prevailed despite the
notorious fact that its enforcement was impracti-
cable. In the year 1700 efforts were again made
by the city definitely to bring about a total exclusion of the Jews. At the same time there was issued
a prohibition against visits by the Oberhausen
Jews. However—and this was the decisive factor

as regarded its practical effectiveness—the "commissioners of the great lords" were not to be affected
by the terms of this prohibition.

The first Jew after Isaac Ulmann to be given the
right to take up his residence in Augsburg as imperial
commissioner, under the decree of March 1700,
was Samuel Moses Ulmann. The powerful Viennese
War Court Factor, Samuel Oppenheimer, was also,
in 1700, accorded permission to reside in the city.
This was an incentive for efforts on the part of less
wealthy Jews. Several of these, in 1701, paid to
the Imperial Bailiff a sum of 400 fl. and secured
thereby not alone admission to the city (subject
of course to the "personal escort"), but the return
by the city of the above-mentioned fee (*Douceur*).
In 1702, the war contractor Josef Guggenheimer
came to the city bringing with him several Jewish
employees, and already in 1709 there is a report to
the effect that these employees had engaged in
municipal land speculations, which was forbidden
by a city ordinance.[245] Prominent as agents of
Samuel Oppenheimer among these employees were
the Jews Daniel Ulmann and Mayer Levi. There
followed in 1703 the admission of Mändle and the
war contractor Abraham Ulmann with his sons
Simon and David. Applications by Löb Jonas of
Kriegshaber,[246] Löw Ulmann of Binswangen and
Elias Ulmann of Pfersee for permission to enter
the city were, however, denied. At this time
(September, 1703) the imperial troops encamped
at Pfersee and, according to report, no Jewish
house was left undamaged.[247] As soon as the

residence of these favored Jews was permanently established, their presence in the city was legalized in 1719 by the enactment of a provision that they should not be required to make payment of entrance fees or be charged with personal escort costs, but should pay for their protection. This was hardly more than a formal revision, clearly revealing the helplessness and embarrassment of the city. The broadening out of Jewish commercial activities in the city is attested by the decision, at the same time, that Jewish bills of exchange were to be registered by the city.

The Christian citizens themselves appeared to be wavering in their deep-rooted, centuries-old conviction that the Jews were harmful to the economic existence of the community. In 1719, the goldsmiths, who had originally participated in recurrent movements aimed at Jewish expulsion, withdrew their signatures from the petition on the ground that in the prevailing troubled times the presence of the Jews as purchasers of their products was of importance to them.[248] On the whole, however, the tradespeople retained their extreme anti-Semitic attitude. They forced the municipal administration in 1706 to a reënactment of the Jewish exclusion order and pursued this illiberal policy uninterruptedly until late in the 19th century.

Following the disintegration of the municipal policy revealed in the enactments of 1719, another attempt was made in 1732 to drive the Jews from

the city. The many services which had in the
meantime been rendered by the Jews during the
exigencies of the war periods enabled them, however, to organize a successful resistance to these
efforts. Jakob Ulmann invoked the intervention
of the Elector of the Palatinate (1732), Oswald
Ulmann and Moses Neuburger that of the Emperor
(1738), in the matter of readmission to the city.
The Jews maintained, and the Emperor and the
Elector agreed with them, that the imperial ratifica-
tions of the Jewish expulsions or exclusions (1456
and 1599) had reference to the right of Jewish
domicile in the city but did not affect the rights of
the Jews to enter the city and have temporary
residence within its precincts. As early as 1718
the Elector had acquiesced in this interpretation
by the Jews.

Foreign Jews also found temporary opportunities of transacting business in the city, when, in
1712–14, the sessions of the Diet were transferred
from Regensburg to Augsburg in consequence of
the pestilence raging at that time. The Counts
Pappenheim also maintained their right of Jewish
escort in opposition to the city of Augsburg.[249]

The efforts made by the kings and rulers on
behalf of the Jews applied in general only to favored
Jewish individuals and rarely to the Jews in the
suburbs of Augsburg as a whole. Even when at
one time in 1732 an effort was made by the King
along these lines, it achieved no lasting results.

The Emperor demanded that the city adopt a "more neighborly attitude" in its relation to the Jews.[250]

To give a detailed report of the frequent variations in the Jewish municipal policy would lead us too far afield in this concise presentation. We must be content to refer to the special literature on this subject, especially the municipal chronicles of the well-informed Councilor Paul von Stetten who was himself active in the administration of the city's Jewish policy. In only a general way can a picture be given here of the helplessness of the city, as revealed in its actions:

(1) In the repeated admission and expulsion of the Jews in general.

(2) In the frequent manifestations of individual discrimination between the Jews who enjoyed a more powerful protection and those who did not.

(3) In the aimless variations affecting the extent of Jewish rights and the compensations exacted for granting them.[251]

Referring to the absurdity of the municipal Jewish policy, Paul von Stetten, in the year 1803, passes the following retrospective judgment:

"Inasmuch as the authorities, either voluntarily or acting under compulsion, permitted the Jews to have access to the city at daytime, it certainly confuses a main issue with an incidental one to have regarded it as important to deny

their presence at night." The police escort, he
adds, "fell into desuetude of itself", as the guards
could easily be made complaisant with a glass
of beer. "They seem to have been in a state of
'preëstablished harmony', forever following a
path that never led to a satisfactory goal".[252]

The city, by reason of its unstable Jewish policy,
came into conflict with all of the interested factions:
(1) its own citizens; (2) the Emperor; (3) the
various ruling powers, above all, the Bishop, the
Imperial Prefect of the Realm, and the administration of the Margravate of Burgau; (4) the Jews
themselves. Conflicts with its own citizens, primarily the jewelers, later also the weavers and
dyers, were precipitated not only by the uninterrupted appeals to the municipal administration
concerning the Jews, but also by the municipal functionaries, some of whom (municipal care-takers and
satellites) were recipients from the Jews of personal
escort fees, New Year's gifts and church consecra-
tion assessments, and feared the loss of this source
of income if the Jews were driven out. The city's
treasurer was at times compelled to make good
these losses.

The contentions between the Emperor and the
city grew out of the fact that the latter was denied
exercise of the sovereignty over Jewish affairs
which had been guaranteed it in the time of Rudolf
in 1599. The Emperor at various times made
regulations in favor of the Jews generally, but in

most instances these were directed to individual cases. In 1641, by order of the Emperor, permission to enter the city was granted to Isaac Ulmann.[253] Such permission was also accorded in 1700 and 1702 to Samuel Moses Ulmann and Josef Guggenheimer, indirectly also to Maier Levi as the representative of Samuel Oppenheimer; in 1703 to Abraham Ulmann and his sons Simon and David; in 1750 to Isaac and Mayer Landauer; in 1774 to Isaac Amschel Goldschmidt. Following an imperial order in 1761 all Jews were denied admission to the city for a period of nine months, under the provisions connected with the operation of the new coinage regulations.

There were difficulties also between the city and other rulers and functionaries. We have already spoken of the efforts of the Imperial Prefect in behalf of Simon Oppenheimer. In the conflict growing out of leadership in the direction of Jewish affairs between Löw Simon Ulmann and Isaac Landauer, there was an injection of authority on the part of the Prefect, as also on the part of the city itself and of a group of other interested Christian functionaries. There is evidence of more frequent intervention by the Bavarian dukes who, having been involved in nearly all the wars of the 17th and 18th centuries, were, in consequence, very much inclined to show favor to the Jews who were in a position to furnish the sinews of war. In 1741, in deference to Bavarian influence, permit of domicile was accorded the business establishment of Abraham Mändle, comprising the privilege

of residence in the city to eight or nine families,
with the reservation indeed that they make their
homes in a public hostelry. After a preliminary
refusal, Mändle was given permission to occupy
a private residence, with a view to ritualistic purposes. His home was in the neighborhood of the
convent of St. Catherine and of the *Collegium
Evangelicum*. Protests were made to the city by
both factions against this Jewish proximity. Ecclesiastical encroachment upon municipal Jewish policy
is again brought to light in these protests. In the
meantime, the position occupied by Mändle was
rendered so strong by the Bavarian protection that
he was even enabled to maintain the tacit toleration of his house of prayer. He, together with
Moses Neuburger, is said to have been arrested on
this account in 1744. A conflict broke out in 1743
between the city and the Bavarian Elector by
reason of his expulsion together with that of other
Jews. The Elector in 1749 demanded that residence in the city be accorded Mändle and his
establishment for an extended period upon the
payment of a fixed assessment, which should not
be subject to change. In 1766 a request was made
by Mändle for the freedom of all the city gates,
in contrast to the restriction placed upon all other
Jews who, for purposes of supervision, were allowed
to enter the city through the Gögginger Gate only.

The city was involved in difficulties on all sides
in connection with a dispute regarding the Jewish
burial ground, these difficulties continuing with
protracted interruptions from 1720 to 1794. This

burial ground, which had been in use since 1627, and was located between the towns of Kriegshaber and Stadtbergen, had grown too small for the community's requirements. Already in 1720 interments were made under the entrance gate. The purchase of an additional tract for the extension of the burial ground was objected to by the dean and chapter of the episcopate as well as by the city, as owners of the adjacent tracts. The Jews intended to erect upon the new land a guardhouse with two dwellings, one of which was to be occupied by a Christian guard to be installed by the Jews in view of the disturbed conditions of the time. In support of their plans for the extension of the burial place and the erection of the guard house they had the coöperation of the Margravate of Burgau, as against the opposition of the city and the Bishop. Among the objections to a Christian guard was the following, that in the event of his death it would be necessary to convey the Christian sacrament into a Jewish cemetery. The building operation which had been instituted with the acquiescence of the Margravate was demolished by the municipal militia in defiance of the law. The building was, however, finally completed with the assent of the Emperor. The municipality had to give way all along the line. But it was not until 1794 that the prosecution instituted against the municipality in connection with the outrage was quashed by imperial clemency. The Bishop, too, participated in

this burial ground dispute, as well as in the dissensions regarding the office of Jewish leader, and,
in general, he was opposed to the political and
economic progress of the Jews, as there was always
a danger of involving matters affecting the Faith.
This however, did not prevent him from favoring,
as did the secular rulers, such Jews as came under
his own jurisdiction. In 1722 he threatened reprisals
against the city for the reason that it had refused
"free passage" to his Jews, i. e. toll-free entrance
to the city, although such was granted to others.
Through the influence of the episcopal authority
admission to the city was also granted the sons of
the episcopal Court-Jew Löw Simon Ulmann, named
Götz and Wolf, who were themselves Court-Jews
in Hohenlohe, and through similar influence, to
the Court-Jew of Bayreuth, Isaac Levi.

Other rulers whose attitude involved the city
in difficulties on account of their Jews included the
Elector of the Palatinate, the Archbishop of
Mayence, the Bishop of Constance, the Princes of
Thurn and Taxis and of Anhalt-Zerbst. The city
was compelled to come to an understanding with
all these favored Jews. "Time and again complaints were lodged with the municipal authorities
that free entrance to the city had been denied to
certain Court-Jews."[254] It even came to the point
that rivalries were provoked between individual
rulers by reason of supposed or actual discrimination between one Court-Jew and another. Though

expressions of this character may merely indicate
the pettiness of the officialdom of the period, there
can be no doubt that the actual achievements of
the Jews who enjoyed the favor of the rulers fully
justified their right to effective protection.[255]

A communication addressed to the municipality
by the Court of Munich in 1745 relates that:

> "These persons have rendered a great service
> and are still doing so, and we shall therefore take
> most effective measures at all times to protect
> them."

In this manner, throughout the entire 17th and
18th centuries, the city was on the one hand subjected to the urgence of its citizens to keep the
"troublesome brood of Jews" at a distance, and
on the other hand it was always compelled by the
rulers, and to a certain extent by its own fiscal
interests, to grant admittance to them, especially
to the commercially influential Jews who were the
most favored by the rulers and the most detested
and feared by the citizens.

In the manifold declarations by the citizens
protesting against the admission of the Jews,
ecclesiastical influences were entirely subordinated
to those of an economic nature. The free commercial activities of the Jews ran distinctly counter
to the economic conception and methods of the
guilds. The Jews, whose special economic conditions
and potentialities in time of war were hardly in
competition with the citizenry, must have been
disturbing to the economic order of the latter in

times of peace. For this reason, after a conclusion of peace, there always followed renewed proposals on the part of the citizenry for their exclusion. This economic policy of the cities would have proven untenable in the period of a newly developing industrialism even if the Jews were kept out. Far from securing their own economic stability by their exclusion of Jews, the townspeople retarded the economic progress of the time, whose leaders included also a number of Jews. This will be clarified when we come to consider the fate of Isaac Amschel Goldschmidt in the sequel.

There are no details available that would throw light upon the commercial activities of the Jesse Ulmann whose admission to the city was directed by the Emperor at the time of the Thirty Years' War. During the war of the Spanish Succession the Hamburg Jew Salomon von der Port came to Augsburg. He is reported, according to charges made by the citizens who were opposed to him, to have lived only by speculation, "inasmuch as he did not regard it as a hazard to risk at one time many thousands of gulden."[256] He traded in jewels and precious metals and is said to have secured a sort of monopoly in this business. He remained in Augsburg for a long period after the conclusion of the war.

More detailed information is furnished in another instance in which a Jew achieved for a time a quasi-monopolistic position in the Augsburg textile industry in opposition to the economic order of the citizens' guilds. Isaac Amschel Goldschmidt of

Kriegshaber had been accorded residence in Augsburg in 1764. He was associated with the Frankfort firm of Isaac Lehmann Hanauer.[257] His business methods violated all the traditional and legally established trade practices. He brought to Augsburg many foreign textiles, especially from Saxony, Swabia, Switzerland and even India, to the impairment of the local market in woven goods—the principal feature of Augsburg's industrial activity—and imported, in addition, wool and dyestuffs, i. e. the raw materials used in the trade, thus infringing upon the rights of various guilds. He often paid the weavers and pressers with imported raw materials instead of cash. The importation of foreign wares, the introduction of what was known at a later date as the "truck-system" in making payments, the importation of raw goods and materials of various kinds through a single channel, and turning it over to the working men as entrepreneurs, all these innovations constituted a violation of law and provoked indignation. While the Christian weaver was required by the regulations to deal only in domestic products, was the Jewish industrialist to be permitted to import foreign wares and, moreover, by making his weavers into wage workers to bring them into a state of dependence, and introduce an illegal method of payment? The antagonism aroused against Goldschmidt was manifested as early as 1757. The attacks upon him were not stressed, however, inasmuch as though his activities had brought losses to a number of Christian weavers, Goldschmidt

had enabled several bankrupt firms to reëstablish
themselves by means of placing orders with them
on the basis of cash payments. The municipality
did more to further the business activities of Goldschmidt than otherwise. In 1771 it gave him a
specific grant to sell raw materials to the weavers,
to manufacture goods in the cotton mills and to
sell dyestuffs to the latter, on the ground that but for
the "Hanau Company" many weavers would have
been ruined. This grant to Goldschmidt was not,
however, voluntary, nor was it based on a careful
study of economic and political principles. In 1770–71
there had been much suffering due to a shortage
of crops, and the privations experienced by the
weavers, whose business had declined for some
time past, were intensified by this crop failure.
The depression continued for some time, resulting,
in 1794, in the so-called Weavers' Revolt. It was
subsequently asserted that the municipal grant to
Goldschmidt had been a forgery, but this is scarcely
likely in so small a city, in which an act of this kind
would surely have become known.[258] In 1774 the
municipal authorities declared that Goldschmidt
should remain undisturbed (*ohnturbirt*) and an
arrangement was finally reached among the groups
concerned that Goldschmidt's contracts be distributed among all the weavers on the basis of their
customary productive capacity, and that Goldschmidt be required to offset the importation of
specified quantities of goods with the purchase of
an appropriate quantity of Augsburg materials.
In 1791 the weavers succeeded in having an order

issued enjoining Goldschmidt from continuing his "Truck-system". The matter was referred to the Emperor—Goldschmidt was imperial Court-Jew—but the procedure and the entire Goldschmidt business were dissolved shortly thereafter upon the breaking out of the war.

A similar fate was experienced by an outstanding Christian competitor of Goldschmidt's, the Augsburg weaver, Heinrich Schüle. His affairs were conducted along similar lines and he was subjected to much opposition. He possessed, however, two decided advantages. In the first place he was a Christian and had grown up as a worker in the weaving trade; moreover, he was himself a practical manufacturer, possessing technical qualifications, whereas Goldschmidt was merely a capable and ingenious businessman. Schüle's financial backer, the Augsburg banker Oberwexer, was one of Goldschmidt's most powerful opponents. That the latter had been able to override the opposition of both Schüle and Oberwexer gives proof of his extraordinary talents. Goldschmidt's annual financial turnovers were in 1774 estimated at 300,000 fl.

We have now presented the picture of two outstanding Augsburg Jewish business men, one in the beginning of the 17th century, the other in the middle of the 18th century, both of whom had grown out of the framework of Jewish commercial activities. For the rest, the trading activities of the Jews in the suburbs of Augsburg appear to have been promoted along the lines of business opportunities, among which are to be included the extended

operations connected with furnishing supplies of
war materials. It lies in the nature of such opportunism in business engagements that they are not
bound by commercial traditions and that they are
more prone to irregular business methods than are
the regularly established trading operations. It is
even reported that several of the Jews who had
found refuge in the city from the dangers of the
prevailing war had devoted themselves to land
speculations. In 1693 they were reproached with
having illegally conducted a trade in gold, silver
and jewelry, which had been forbidden them by the
Swabian provincial administration. In 1708 it is
reported that the Fugger Palace Market was
burglarized for the benefit of Jewish traders. In
1728 there is reference to an arrest of the brothers
Kitzinger on the charge of having been purchasers
of stolen copper. In 1741 there followed, on charges
of similar offenses, the arrest of Süsskind Oppenheimer and Rahel Landauer, and in 1791 the Jewish
Beadle, Wolf Moses, was caught in the act of steal-
ing silver pieces. All the foregoing had come from
Pfersee. Jewish goldsmiths are charged with having
been fraudulently engaged in the production of
alloyed silver.[259] In 1714, a usurious Jew (Josef
Kitzinger) is reported to have exacted, despite the
security of his pledges, a yearly interest of 24%,
30%, even as high as 120% upon loans advanced
by him. In 1754, Herz Levi was also charged with
usury. In 1726, Samuel Kohn of Kriegshaber was
charged with the sale of imitation silver; and in
1743, Oswald Ulmann was accused of having

swindled a Christian widow of Augsburg out of her fancy-goods business. Charges were not infrequently brought against the Jews for trading with devalued coinage. All these transgressions are reported by enemies of the Jews and all accusations are, therefore, not to be accorded too ready a credence. At the same time, there is no reason for doubting all these charges. By reason of far-reaching repressions, the Jews were provoked to a certain lack of scruple and their social degradation robbed them of many natural restraints. The barriers between moral and legal prohibitions might at times have become uncertain. There is recorded, however, in 1804, an incident of a sinister nature. Charges of counterfeiting were brought by a young converted Jew, Löb Ulmann, against his father and a group of Jews residing in the Augsburg Suburbs. The accused were taken into custody on Yom Kippur in the synagogue and held in confinement for a long time, until their innocence was proved.[260]

When it is considered that the above-mentioned accusations covered a lengthy period of time and were distributed throughout a rather extended sphere of population, it is clear that they do not imply a widespread criminality. Instructive in this connection is the circumstance that after the middle of the 18th century, with the improved social and economic condition of the Jews, charges of moral delinquencies among them practically ceased, and the only complaints we hear of are of their competition in business. This is the more significant inasmuch as until far into the 19th

century, the trading of the majority of Jews was
restricted to "rags, bones, old clothes, common
farm horses, coarse peasant cloth and similar
material of little value".[261] That these legal restrictions confined the commercial activities of the
Jews to country districts is proved by the character
of the above-mentioned articles of trade. This
constituted the so-called Peddling (*Schacher*) or
Jewish trading with the country folk. This Jewish
trading was stigmatized as most deplorable in
numerous memorials when, a half century later,
the Bavarian government, at the time of the Montgelas ministry, instituted an energetic reform
policy. Within a constricted terrain there were
crowded about 100 Jewish families, all striving for
a livelihood in dealing in the few permitted articles
of trade, all restricted to a rural clientele, which
was, in the main, similarly trammeled, similarly
insecure in their livelihood, and leading an equally
pitiful existence. There are no specific details at
hand regarding the petty peddling activities of these
Jews. It is hardly conceivable that this striving
for a meager subsistence could have always been
carried on in strict conformity with the hard rigors
of the law.

The number of those Jews who, in contrast to
the impoverished peddlers, occupied well-paying
posts as court-agents and war-contractors, together
with those participating as functionaries in these
profitable enterprises, was relatively small. They
were not, however, so very few in number, inasmuch
as the recurring wars and the large number of

sovereigns of petty German principalities tended to cultivate their usefulness, and the Jews had only to utilize as much as possible the opportunities provided by the exigencies of war. Their most profitable business ventures were undertaken at times when the state of war brought with it an abeyance of many prohibitions.[262] The commercial morale of peace times could not therefore be expected of them.

They were, in times of peace, engaged mainly in trading in precious and other metals and grain stuffs. Their business relations with members of opulent circles favored especially their trading in jewelry. We have seen above that the Christian jewelers of Augsburg declared, in 1719, that their business would suffer ruin if the Jews were expelled from the city.[263] We must consider in this connection not only the improvement of the business market due to the Jews, but also their importance in the procuring of raw materials through their well known connections with the commercial circles of Frankfort, Hamburg and Amsterdam.[264]

The drastic changes evoked by the wars, in contrast to the practices obtaining in times of peace, can be seen in the fact that in 1716 the city of Augsburg itself bought iron from the Jews for the manufacture of cannon. The Christian dealers naturally objected.[265] In the second half of the 18th century the Jewish trade in jewelry and metals was subordinated to the textile industry. This was the beginning of the Jewish association with the commercial tradition of the city. Until this time

the Jews had been explicitly excluded from participation in the textile trade, and the expansion of
their commercial activities by the inclusion of this
industry marks a radical change in the long established German economic conception.

On the other hand, another industry of the Jews
went back to an old Jewish economic tradition,
namely dealing in horses, which had been carried
on on a large scale by the Jews in the Augsburg
suburbs as a result of the wars that raged in the
eighteenth century. In the War of the Spanish
Succession, Josef Mändle and Joseph Neuburger
are mentioned as commissioners for the purchase of
horses for the army. Oswald Ulmann furnished
horses for the imperial cavalry. The most extended
operations in this line appear to have been conducted by Abraham Mändle during the Seven
Years' War. As early as 1696 the city had taken
steps to levy a sales tax on horse-dealing operations
by Jews. The supply of forage was naturally associated with the supply of horses. As the agent of
Samuel Oppenheimer, it is reported that David
Ulmann of Pfersee alone had purchased for the
troops of Prince Eugene, in the year 1701, 20,000
cwt. of flour, 100,000 cwt. of hay, 160,000 cwt. of
oats, 180,000 cwt. of meat and 15,000 quarts of
wine. The materials furnished by Abraham Mändle
for the campaign of 1757 are said to have covered
the entire commissary requirements of the Bavarian
contingent in bread, hay, straw and wood. He also
negotiated the forage supplies for the fortresses of
Breisach, Kehl and Philippsburg. In 1759, he was

again active for a brief period as war-contractor
after having for a time been replaced by a Christian.
The latter, however, was not able to dispense
entirely with Jewish coöperation, having engaged
the services of Isaac Levi of Kriegshaber, the
Landauer brothers and Ulmann.

The war-contracting activities, too, represented
a phase of business opportunism, and one that was
of a distinctly speculative character. The debtors
in these transactions, both cities and rulers, had
themselves grown impoverished through the disturbances of war times and other circumstances. Thus
the government of Bavaria remained for a number
of decades indebted to Abraham Mändle, who continued to furnish horses for the State until about
1778, well into the times of peace. He was finally
compelled to enter suit for his claims against the
State, as was the case with the family of Samuel
Oppenheimer against Austria. In the end the
widow lost her case and died in poverty in old age.

In contrast to these occasional business activities,
small and great, the traditional banking and money
exchange business of the Jews was definitely ham-
pered by stringent prohibitory enactments of the
city. In the 17th century the city had endeavored
to restrict business of this nature by requiring the
Jews to pay for the privilege of residence according
to the length of the stay. In 1719 it was decided
that Jewish bills of exchange would be valid only
upon official registration,[266] and in 1735 the city
authorities declared that bills of exchange upon
Jews could be issued only by married persons who

reached the age of 25 years. In 1802 the citizenry
tried to enact a law that all bills of exchange issued
by Jews not resident in Augsburg should be protested. This effort was rendered futile through the
intervention of the Elector of Bavaria. In 1803
the citizens demanded that all Jewish bills of exchange be made payable by gentile citizens.[267]
In the meantime, in this period of advancement,
the municipal administration refused to yield to
the pressure of the citizens, but appealed to the
imperial administration in Vienna for an opinion
(*Merkantilparere*) regarding the expediency of foreign bills of exchange. The contention pro and
con involved not only the interests of the Jews but
those of foreigners in general. The decision was in
favor of foreign bills of exchange, as had been
anticipated by the city. The city was not, however,
able to evade the rather unreasonable demand that
Jewish debts on bills of exchange be made payable
in the morning, while claims by Jews on bills of
exchange be payable in the afternoon. This provision, too, affected not only the Jews, but all
strangers, though it was primarily aimed at the
Jews. The Councilor Paul von Stetten makes this
reference to the matter:—"This enactment was
never put into practical operation. Only occasionally is it advanced by one merchant or another for
the purpose of annoying the Jew. The Burgomaster's functionaries, however, come to the support of the latter on these occasions".[268] The circumstance that the Jews with the exception of those
who were privileged (*Akkordjuden*) were prevented

from maintaining a writing room or office in the city had as a consequence that Jewish bills of exchange debts had to be brought to the creditor (*Bringschulden*). The provisions of the Augsburg bill of exchange enactments of 1716 and 1778 remained, however, fundamentally effective.

The numerous laws in this matter evidence the widespread Jewish transactions in bills of exchange. The circumstances lead to the presumption that down to about the middle of the 18th century—with the exception of the war periods—bills of exchange based on credit predominated, whereas later those based on sale of merchandise were in the ascendency. This presumption is supported by the above-mentioned enactment of 1735, the purpose of which was to prevent the borrowing of money from Jews by thoughtless young people in defiance of the existing prohibition. Clearer evidence of the correctness of this presumption lies in the increase of Jewish commercial activities following the middle of the century.

Little is known of the private credit business of the Jews in that period, which had to be carried on secretly in consequence of the municipal enactments. Regarding the commercial activities of the Jews, complaint was made that owing to the establishing of lower prices by them, Christian merchants were disadvantageously affected. It was contended that the Jews, who were not permitted to maintain business establishments, were able to carry on their trading at a smaller operating expense. It is doubtful, however, whether this advantage was not offset by the substantial imposts exacted from them by the various rulers, above all by the numerous claims made upon them by the municipality itself. Added to this was the fact that, at any rate until the turn of the century, Jewish petty trading was restricted to the annual fairs, at which low prices always prevailed. It was ordered by the city in 1735 that Jews be permitted to dispose of their wares only at these annual fairs. The mitigation of the rigid Jewish restrictive laws began with an enactment in 1791, when it was decreed that the Jews, even though not permitted to maintain shops, be allowed to own repositories for the storing of their wares.[269]

As fluctuating as were the commercial activities of the Jews so was their number. The census was taken periodically for the purpose of tax levies. In Pfersee there were 18 to 20 Jewish householders recorded at the end of the 17th century, representing with family and attendants a population of about 150 individuals.[270] The Jewish community of Kriegshaber is reported to have increased tenfold between 1653 and 1722, from six or seven families to sixty or seventy. The total number of families in 1704 is given as 62.[271] In 1732, the Kriegshaber census records the presence of 402 Jewish persons; in Kriegshaber, Pfersee and Steppach altogether, 61 householding families. The tax records of Pfersee reveal the presence there in 1721 of 76 Jews liable to payment of the coronation tax, i. e. all those Jews who were over thirteen years of age. In 1803, the total number of Jewish families is given as 116. A closer examination of these imposts shows the presence of Jews in Pfersee as 76 over the age of 13 years (1721), which would make a Jewish population of at least 150 persons. In a further consideration of the above-given enumeration in Kriegshaber in 1732, we may assume a total population of about 1000 individuals. The total population of 61 families in 1732, of which not more than one half, probably less, can be accredited to Kriegshaber, indicates that this would be a large number of persons per family. It is necessary, therefore, to put a figure of 700 persons upon the recorded presence of 61 families. There would remain, then, a total of about 300 persons, including unrecorded residents, uncounted poor persons and students, and fluctuating elements. The latter were known to be quite numerous in the Germany of the 18th century. That there was contact of the Jews in the suburban towns of Augsburg with the great reservoir of Eastern Europe, in which these elements had their origin, is evidenced in the participation by the Jews of Augsburg, in 1745, in a movement on behalf of Jews who had been driven out of Bohemia.[272]

The internal conditions of the Jewish communities can hardly be described as stable in view of the unsettled state of the times and the questionable nature of the prevailing living conditions. The situation of the Jews was in direct contrast to that of the Christian citizens. If the latter maintained with unyielding rigidity the medieval structure of economic affairs, the Jews, on the contrary, until far into the 19th century, were unable to attain, after the upheavals affecting their living conditions during the Middle Ages, any sound political, economic or social order of existence. In the course of the 18th century, the older families, especially such as the Ulmanns, the Kitzingers, the Neuburgers, found themselves relegated to a subordinate place within the Jewish fold. A violent conflict was precipitated between Löw Simon Ulmann, head of the Pfersee Jewry from 1722 to 1764, and Isaac Landauer, to secure leadership in Jewish affairs. Ulmann had known how to maintain his supremacy throughout a span of years, as he had secured the support of the Bishop and of the Superior Bailif of Burgau. In the ensuing contest he was, at the instance of his opponents, subjected to the payment of a fine by the high prefect of the city for having refused to acquiesce in a regular election. Eventually, through the efforts of the newly elected Chief Rabbi of Swabia, the contending factions agreed to acknowledge the leadership of Ulmann. There is here revealed the spirit of the "absolutism of the period". This spirit is also revealed in the methods adopted in this conflict. Ulmann characterized his opponent as a "rebel" and an "impertinent and coarse buffoon and arch-liar".

The precarious condition of the Jews justified to a certain extent an autocratic rulership. This is exemplified in the long-drawn-out conflict in the matter of the Jewish burial ground.[273] In contentions of this nature the Jews could succeed only through the intervention of influential leaders with their protectors. Disastrous consequences of these

autocratic regimes were avoided in part by the
constricted sphere of Jewish autonomy, and partly
by the strong ties which bound the Jews to their
religion. There is no indication that the organs of
the autonomous administration which functioned
in judicial, ritual and tax-levying matters, seriously
misused these powers. It must be borne in mind
that in the 18th century, in contrast to the condition
prevailing at a later period, even the Jews of high
standing attached great importance to the traditional Jewish concepts and mode of life. It was
not until the middle of the 18th century that in
Augsburg as well as in other places the first signs
of the change began to show themselves in the form
of an appreciation of German secular culture.
Abraham Mändle had engaged for his children the
services of a Christian tutor for the study of the
German language and elementary subjects.[274]

THE 19TH CENTURY

IF the successful Jewish merchants were the first
to recognize the utility of a German secular educa-
tion in the practical affairs of life, it was they, too,
who promoted the removal of Jewish restrictions.
In Augsburg the idealistic interests which favored
the Jewish emancipation were clearly associated
with economic interests.

The Jewish emancipation movement found at
the beginning of the century two strong supporters
among the leaders of the Augsburg municipal

administration: Senator Paul von Stetten and the
State Councilor Hoscher. The proposals of the
former were predicated entirely upon practical
considerations, as already indicated in the citations.
His most important proposal was to the effect that
while the Jews were fundamentally entitled to
rights of domicile in the city, these rights should
be conditioned upon the possession of 30,000 to
40,000 florins.[275] He also suggested that Jews be
permitted the purchase of land, but be, at the same
time, made to purchase secularized properties of
the Church which swamped the real estate market
and were in consequence difficult to dispose of.
Hoscher, on the contrary, based his advocacy of
Jewish emancipation upon more idealistic considerations, defining his attitude as being "for the purpose of removing old prejudices".

Decisive in the success of this movement were,
however, neither the political nor the idealistic
considerations, but the fiscal interest of the municipality. In the year 1803 there was a maturing
municipal indebtedness on bills of exchange amounting, respectively, to 33,600 and 113,040 florins
owing to the bank of Veit Kaulla of Kriegshaber
and the associated banks of Jakob Obermeyer and
Kaulla. The municipality had been reluctant to
turn to the Jews for the loan of these moneys that
would in part, at any rate, have been diverted to
Paris to secure, through Napoleon, the continuance
of the municipal sovereignty. It had endeavored
at first to negotiate these loans with the state bank
of Hesse-Cassel and with Frankfort Christian bank-

ers. These loans bore no interest and only after
the expiration of the third year was there to be an
interest charge of 5%. This represented an unintentional repetition of a well-known medieval situation.
The city was enabled with the money secured from
the Jews to further its political interests, and this
served at the same time to strengthen the legal
position of the Jews. From this time on the city
gave the Jews also the conventional title "Mister"
(*Herr*), whereas the designation "Jew" (*Yud*) had
been formerly used in all official relations. This
improvement came suddenly. As recently as 1796,
in the war period, the city had refused to accord
the Jews even emergency quarters and had expelled
those who had come in anyhow. In 1799–1800,
when Augsburg was the headquarters of the war-
commission, there followed a renewed influx of
Jews, at which time there came to Augsburg among
others, Hirsch Wolf Levi (nau), who was accorded
citizenship rights in 1814. There was still present
the tendency to Jewish expulsion. Pressure to this
end was still exerted by the citizenry, unchanged
in the passing of the centuries, protesting that they
could not understand "how the high authorities of
the land could look with such unconcern upon the
spoliation of one after the other of their fellow
citizens by this deceitful brood".[276] It was even
suggested that the Kosher restaurant (*Garküche*)
be suppressed, although this suggestion was eventually dropped out of consideration for the specially
favored Jews, as had been the case in former times.
When, however, in 1803, several Jews declared

themselves ready to assist the city treasury in every
way possible (*"in das aerarium quaevis praestanda
zu praestiren"*), the fiscal interests of the city prevailed. Domiciliary rights were granted the impe-
rially-protected Jews and the favored Jews of
Augsburg (*"die Kaiserlichen Schutz- und Augsburger Akkordjuden"*) Jakob Obermayer, Simon
Wallersteiner, Henle Ephraim Ulmann and the
Munich bankers Strasburger and Westheimer.
This grant was, however, restricted by the inclusion
of a number of provisos: the Jews were not to have
a synagogue, engage in no retail trading, bring into
the city not more than one grown-up child possessing at least 30,000 florins, and pay a "recognition
fee". This was fixed in the case of Obermayer at
250 florins, of Ulmann at 350 fl., of Strasburger
and Westheimer at 750 fl. annually. Obermayer
took up his residence in Domherrenhof, the later
residence of the first Burgomaster of the city. This
marks a reversal of former conditions. The Jews
had previously been permitted lodgment only in
public hostelries or with small tradespeople on the
occasion of temporary visits to the city. These
lodgments were mostly in the Anna Strasse, on
the Schwall, at the upper Moat, by the Brunnlech
and similar places. It never occurred to these
successful merchants to make use of their influence
in favor of improving the legal status of the Jews
in the Augsburg suburbs generally. They contented
themselves with the personal advantages they had
secured, and their main concern was that no other
Jews should become their competitors by being

given rights similar to theirs. They protested against the admission of newcomers to the city. Despite this attitude on their part, the Christian citizens at first objected even to the rights of domicile which had been granted the successful Jewish merchants themselves, declaring that "a great fuss is made these days about tolerance, but it is badly understood and is not at all suitable for our restricted domain, nay it is impossible, and will completely destroy the welfare and livelihood of our citizens".

There was no time left to determine whether the fears of the citizens regarding the Jewish menace were well founded, for despite the funds that had been expended in Paris in 1803, the "constricted domain" of Augsburg passed out of existence within a short time, the city being incorporated with the Bavarian state in 1806. The moderately liberal Jewish policy adopted by the Montgelas ministry, which was closely related in spirit to the proposals of von Stetten, was consequently carried into effect in Augsburg also, and the independent Jewish policy of this city thus came to an end after an existence of fully 600 years.

After 1806, the Jews who were entitled to domicile were officially designated as "the royally protected and authorized Jews in the city of Augsburg". In 1807, consequent upon commercial depressions and losses, the "recognition fee" paid by Ulmann was reduced. In 1809, it was fixed at the uniform

amount of 25 florins, with the understanding that
after the death of those liable to this impost, it
should be discontinued. This constituted a still
farther advance toward granting them the rights
of citizenship. In 1809, there were 56 Jews residing
in the city, in a population of almost 30,000 Christians. It was a modest number.

The Jews are said to have been unofficially permitted to maintain a Hall of Prayer in the city at
that time. It is reported that in the synagogue of
Kriegshaber the visitors were warned against attending the Obermayer House of Prayer. In 1814, in
consequence of the Bavarian Jewish edict of the
previous year, the Jews were granted the rights of
citizenship. At the same time official sanction was
given to the establishment of the Hall of Prayer.
As the first incumbent of this pulpit, Rabbi Phinehas
Skutsch of Kriegshaber took the civic oath of
office before the King.

In the course of the 19th century, the local
history of the Augsburg Jewry, as was the case
with that of Regensburg, reveals a continuing
decadence. With the inclusion of the city in the
Bavarian domain and the completion of the Jewish
emancipation, all distinctive municipal and Jewish
development ceased. The specifically Jewish cultural values became more and more absorbed in the
dominating world of German culture.[277] If in the
middle of the 18th century the fewest Jews were
capable of reading and writing the *German* language,

they relinquished, in the hundred years that followed, acquaintance with *Hebraic* learning in speech and writing. Since the beginning of the 20th century there have been indications of a faint-hearted change. This development has been powerfully influenced by the German revolutions of 1918 and 1933. The decadence of Jewish existence in the 19th century will only be properly judged and appraised in a later period, when the ultimate goal to which the destiny of the Jews is leading them becomes clearer to our vision.

NOTES

NOTES

[1] Straus II, 46 ff.

[2] Ib. 44.

[3] See below.

[4] Ms. of the State Library of Munich: Cgm 3022, fol. 3.

[5] Straus I.

[6] Ib. No. 112.

[7] J. Aronius, *Regesten zur Geschichte der Juden im fränkischen und deutschen Reiche bis zum Jahre* 1273 (1902), No. 387.

[8] Straus I.

[9] *Zeitschrift für die Geschichte der Juden in Deutschland*, V (1892), p. 115.

[10] Straus, *Materialien*. Cf. A. Pinthus in *Zeitschrift für die Geschichte der Juden in Deutschland* (N.S.), II (1930), p. 111 ff.

[11] Aronius, l. c., No. 118.

[12] Ib. No. 446.

[13] Straus I.

[14] C. J. W. Wagenseil, *Versuch einer Geschichte der Stadt Augsburg* (1820), vol. I, p. 239. Cf. Ms. of the State Library of Munich, Clm 167, fol. 98b.

[15] Straus II, p. 23.

[16] Straus I.

[17] M. Wiener, *Regesten zur Geschichte der Juden in Deutschland während des Mittelalters* (1862), p. 40, Nos. 111 and 128.

[18] Straus I, No. 567.

[19] Straus II, p. 113.

[20] F. L. Steinthal, *Geschichte der Augsburger Juden im Mittelalter* (1911), p. 15.

[21] Aronius, l. c., No. 203.

[22] See note 17.

[23] Straus I.

[24] Aronius, l. c., No. 618.

[25] Cf. Straus II, p. 82 ff.

[26] Ib., p. 94 ff.

[27] Straus I, No. 693, etc.

[28] Ib. No. 211.

[29] Ib. No. 111.

[30] *Zeitschrift für die Geschichte der Juden in Deutschland* (N.S.), III (1931), p. 280.

[31] M. von Freyberg, *Sammlung historischer Schriften und Urkunden* (1836 ff.), II, p. 350.

[32] Straus I.

[33] J. Mayer, in *Deutsch-israelitische Zeitung*, passim.

[34] See below.

[35] Further details in H. Ehrentreu in *Jahrbuch der jüdisch-literarischen Gesellschaft*, III (1905), p. 206 ff.

[36] Mose Minz, *Responsa* 19, and Maharil, *Minhagim*, fol. 89a.

[37] See below.

[38] Straus, *Materialien*.

[39] Straus II, p. 47 ff.

[40] See below.

[41] On the following cf. A. Freimann in *Monatsschrift der Gesellschaft zur Förderung der Wissenschaft des Judentums*, XVII (1909), p. 589 ff.

[42] I. Elbogen, *Der jüdische Gottesdienst in seiner geschichtlichen Entwicklung* (1913), p. 335; L. Zunz, *Literaturgeschichte der synagogalen Poesie* (1866), p. 250.

[43] L. Zunz, *Die synagogale Poesie des Mittelalters* (Reprint 1920), p. 254.

[44] *Germania Judaica* (1934), p. 290.

[45] Straus II, p. 101.

[46] L. Zunz, *Gesammelte Schriften* (1874), I, p. 169; *Germania Judaica*, p. 291.

[47] Schmetzer, in *Zeitschrift für die Geschichte der Juden in Deutschland*, III (1931), p. 22; Krautheimer, *Mittelalterliche Synagogen*, p. 177 ff.

[48] According to the extracts by Zunz, Güdemann, Dubnow.

[49] Israel Bruna, *Responsa*, and others.

[50] H. Graetz, *Geschichte der Juden*, VIII (1864), p. 209.

[51] Illustration in *Festschrift zum 70. Geburtstag von A. Berliner* (1903), p. 193, better in A. Kohut, *Geschichte der deutschen Juden*, p. 485.

[52] Gotthard Deutsch, *Israel of Bruna*, Boston, 1908.

[53] Straus I, No. 13.

[54] Ib. No. 149. Cf. "Beiträge zur Geschichte der Juden" in *Festschrift zum 70. Geburtstag von M. Philippson* (1916), p. 82.

[55] Graetz, l. c., p. 223.

[56] Straus II, passim.

[57] Reported by Wülfer in his translation of Brenzsch's *Schlangenbalg*, Nuremberg, 1681.

[58] *Leket Yosher*, of Joseph b. Moses, ed. J. Freimann, 1903/04.

[59] Graetz, l. c., p. 219.

[60] *Responsa*, passim.

[61] The so called "Pfersee Talmud" escaped the censors, and is therefore of rare value on account of its completeness. It was written in Germany about 1343 and came, after having been in

the temporary possession of Italian and French Jews, to Swabia, where it was in the hands of the Ulma family, many members of which resided in the Augsburg suburbs. From there it came into the possession of the monasteries, and finally, in 1806, into the hands of the Bavarian State (cf. Rabbinowicz, in *Dikduke Soferim*, 1).

[62] Finally, though with reservations, S. Levi in *Zeitschrift für die Geschichte der Juden in Deutschland*, I (1929), p. 24 ff.

[63] Kohut, l. c., p. 727; M. Kayserling, in *Monatsschrift der Gesellschaft zur Förderung der Wissenschaft des Judentums*, 1867.

[64] Before this time the Jews of Regensburg buried their dead in the cemetery at Pappenheim. For this and the following cf. J. Mayer, *Zur Geschichte der Juden in Regensburg* (1913).

[65] Cf. *Allgemeine Zeitung des Judentums* (1871), p. 253.

[66] Aronius, l. c., p. 135.

[67] Brutzkus, in *Zeitschrift für die Geschichte der Juden in Deutschland*, III (1931), p. 100.

[68] Schiffman, in *Zeitschrift*, etc., III (1931), p. 50. Cf. *Monatsschrift*, etc. XVII (1909), p. 590; Aronius, l. c., No. 204.

[69] Aronius, l. c., No. 279.

[70] Ib., No. 314a.

[71] Ib., No. 374.

[72] Ib., No. 582.

[73] *Monatsschrift*, etc. (1909), p. 602.

[74] Straus I.

[75] Aronius, l. c., No. 459.

[76] Ib., No. 708.

[77] Straus II, p. 49.

[78] H. Fischer, *Die verfassungsrechtliche Stellung der Juden in den deutschen Städten während des 13. Jhdts.* (1931), p. 172 ff.

[79] Straus, *Materialien*.

[80] Aronius, l. c., No. 725.

[81] See above.

[82] Illustrations in J. Mayer, *Zur Geschichte der Juden in Regensburg*; also in Altmann, *Geschichte der Juden in Salzburg*, I, p. 64, and in Grünfeld, *Ein Gang durch die Geschichte der Juden in Augsburg* (1912).

[83] Regensburg Register (*Monumenta Boica*, vol. LVII), Nos. 148, 156, 177a, etc.

[84] M. Wiener, l. c., Nos. 59 and 67, respectively.

[85] Regensburg Register, Nos. 418, 424.

[86] Ib.

[87] M. von Freyberg, l. c., pp. 5, 87.

[88] Regensburg Register, No. 833 ff.

[89] Ib., No. 526 ff.

[90] Straus, *Materialien* (Annotation of the municipal secretary: "*War dass er des schuldig sei, dass er sterb als ein Christ; sei aber dass er des unschuldig, dass er sterb als ein frommer Jud*").

[91] Regensburg Register, No. 799.

[92] Straus, *Materialien*.

[93] Ib.

[94] Regensburg Register, No. 848.

[95] See below.

[96] Straus, *Materialien*.

[97] Straus II, p. 83.

[98] The name is always written clearly as "Gnendl" (of Czech origin?). The reading "Guendl" (Janner, *Geschichte der Bischöfe von Regensburg*) is incorrect.

[99] Straus, *Materialien*.

[100] Perhaps also with the "Meister Jacob", who was engaged in numerous financial operations in Munich.

[101] Straus, *Materialien*.

[102] Ib.

[103] Ib.

[104] Ib.

[105] M. Wiener, l. c., p. 139, No. 270.

[106] Niese, in *Historische Zeitschrift*, CI, p. 117.

[107] Straus, *Materialien*.

[108] Ib.; also A. Suessmann, *Die Judenschuldentilgungen unter König Wenzel* (1907).

[109] A. Suessmann, l. c., p. 148.

[110] Straus, *Materialien*.

[111] M. Wiener, l. c., p. 157, No. 367.

[112] Straus, *Materialien*.

[113] Cf. Straus II, p. 48 ff.

[114] Straus, *Materialien*.

[115] Straus II, p. 49.

[116] Straus, *Materialien*.

[117] M. Wiener, l. c., p. 160, No. 391 ff.

[118] Straus, *Materialien*.

[119] Ib.

[120] See above.

[121] Straus, *Materialien*, also Straus II, p. 83.

[122] Ib.

[123] Ib.

[124] L. Zunz, *Synagogale Poesie des Mittelalters*, p. 48.

[125] Ms. of the State Library of Munich, Clm 167, fol. 95.

[126] See note 117.

[127] M. Stern, *König Ruprecht von der Pfalz in seinen Beziehungen zu den Juden* (1898). The unpublished passages used in the sequel are missing there.

[128] Straus, *Materialien*.

[129] Ib.

[130] Ib.

[131] M. Wiener, l. c., p. 167, No. 454.

[132] Straus, *Materialien*.

[133] Ib.

[134] Ib.

[135] Ib.

[136] Ib.

[137] M. Wiener, l. c., p. 174, No. 479.

[138] Ib. p. 175, No. 487.

[139] Straus, *Materialien*.

[140] Ib.

[141] Ib. Cf. M. Wiener, l. c., p. 190, No. 559.

[142] Straus, *Materialien*.

[143] Ib.

[144] Ib.

[145] Ib.

[146] Ib.

[147] Ib.

[148] Straus, in *Zeitschrift für die Geschichte der Juden in Deutschland*, I (1929), p. 96 ff.

[149] M. Wiener, l. c., p. 193, No. 578; *Zeitschrift für die Geschichte der Juden in Deutschland*, III (1889), p. 123.

[150] Incomplete in M. Wiener, l. c., p. 193, No. 581.

[151] See above.

[152] M. Wiener, l. c., p. 79, No. 10.

[153] Ib. p. 81, No. 22.

[154] Straus I, Nos. 74, 79.

[155] Ib. Nos. 156 ff., 173 ff., 183.

[156] See below.

[157] Straus, *Materialien*.

[158] Straus I, Nos. 5 ff., 8, 10.

[159] Straus, *Materialien*.

[160] Ib.

[161] The letters of protection are preserved and attested almost without gaps from 1465 on only. The literature (Gemeiner) erroneously carries the grant of protection for the term of a year back into the 14th century.

[162] Straus, *Materialien*.

[163] Straus I, Nos. 10, 38, 60, 138, 206, 213, 118, 64.

[164] Straus I, Nos. 13, 169 ff. On the vicissitudes of Israel, cf. Graetz, l. c., VIII. He can be proved to have been in Regensburg as early as 1446, not 1456 (Güdemann, *Geschichte des Erziehungswesens*, III, p. 21).

[165] Regensburg Register, No. 462; Straus I, Nos. 46, 48, 53 ff. and passim.

[166] I. e. Jewish students or scholars. *"schalenzen"* = to wander. Güdemann erroneously connects *"Schalantjuden"* with *"Schalent"*, the Sabbath meal.

[167] Straus I, Nos. 46, 48, 53 ff., 140, 168, 211, etc.

[168] C. Th. Gemeiner, *Regensburgische Chronik*, III, p. 931.

[169] I. Kracauer, *Urkundenbuch zur Geschichte der Juden in Frankfurt am Main* (1914), passim.

[170] See above.

[171] Straus II, p. 25.

[172] Straus I, No. 110.

[173] Straus II, p. 38.

[174] A special presentation based on unpublished sources in the Vienna Journal *Menorah*, December, 1928.

[175] Straus I, Nos. 567, 595 ff., 599, 604, etc.

[176] Straus II, p. 66; Gemeiner, l. c., IV, p. 144.

[177] Straus I, No. 676.

[178] Ib. No. 563.

[179] Ib. Nos. 588, 644.

[180] Ib. in the proper place.

[181] The "wealthy Mosse", Mendel von Eger, Pinman (= Benjamin) von Freystadt. Cf. Straus II, p. 102.

[182] Straus II, p. 66.

[183] Straus, *Materialien*.

[184] Ib.

[185] P. Carpzov, *In legem reg. comm.* (1640), p. 677.

[186] Schudt, *Jüd. Merckwürdigkeiten* (1715), IV, p. 233.

[187] *Deutsch-israelitische Zeitung*, vol. XLI, No. 7.

[188] L. Zunz, *Die Synagogale Poesie des Mittelalters*, p. 350.

[189] *Deutsch-israelitische Zeitung*, l. c., No. 9.

[190] Scheppler, *Ueber die Aufhebung des Judenleibzolls* (1805), p. 82.

[191] A. Eckstein, *Der Kampf der Juden um die Emanzipation* (1905), p. 115.

[192] I. Gotthelf, *Die Rechtsvesrhältnisse der Juden in Bayern auf Grundlage der neuesten bayerischen Gesetze* (1852), p. 169.

[193] Aronius, l. c., No. 387.

[194] M. Brück, *Rabbinische Zeremonialgebräuche* (1837), p. 81.

[195] Aronius, l. c., No. 474.

[196] I. Schwalm, in *Neues Archiv für ältere deutsche Geschichts-kunde*, XXIII.

[197] F. Reinertshofer, *Die Steuern und Abgaben der Juden in Augsburg* (Würzburg Dissertation, 1921), p. 24.

[198] Aronius, l. c., No. 641.

[199] M. Wiener, l. c., p. 109, No. 38.

[200] Ib. p. 36, No. 86.

[201] P. von Stetten, *Geschichte der freien Reichsstadt Augsburg* (1745), I, p. 80.

[202] M. Wiener, l. c., p. 212, No. 42. Also *Augsburger Abend-zeitung*, No. 49.

[203] P. von Stetten, l. c., I, p. 89.

[204] R. Gruenfeld, *Ein Gang durch die Geschichte der Juden in Augsburg* (1912), p. 9.

[205] M. Wiener, l. c., p. 110, No. 46.

[206] L. F. Steinthal, *Geschichte der Augsburger Juden in Mittel-alter* (1911), p. 58.

[207] Reinertshofer, l. c., p. 32.

[208] Schudt, l. c., II.1, p. 289; M. Wiener, l. c., pp. 122, 124, 137, Nos. 145, 165, 183.

[209] M. Wiener, l. c., pp. 32 ff., Nos. 56, 63.

[210] Ib. p. 40, No. 111. The *"Trostbriefe"* which the Jews were compelled to return can only be interpreted as "Letters of Con-solation" promising to repay debts due, combined with a promise of protection.

[211] M. Wiener, l. c., p. 127, No. 183.

[212] Ib. p. 130, No. 203.

[213] Ib. p. 135, No. 227.

[214] Ib. p. 134, No. 233.

[215] Ib. pp. 33 and 135, Nos. 63 and 242.

[216] Gruenfeld, l. c., p. 14.

[217] Ib. p. 26. "Jud" is not infrequently found as a proper name of a Christian. Cf. *Zeitschrift für die Geschichte der Juden in Deutschland*, III (1931), p. 130.

[218] חזקיה המכונה הרטמן. Illustration in Grünfeld, l. c., p. 20.

[219] *Zeitschrift des Historischen Vereins für Schwaben und Neu-burg*, IV, p. 216.

[220] P. von Stetten, l. c., I, p. 123. Mention should also be made here of the loan interdiction applied to brokers: Stetten, p. 140.

[221] Steinthal, l. c., p. 37.

[222] According to Reinertshofer, l. c., passim and Steinthal, pp. 27, 38.

[223] M. Wiener, l. c., p. 56, No. 20.

[224] Steinthal is wrong in supposing that half of the Jewish taxes amounted to 2800 fl. and the whole tax therefore to 5600 fl. This is impossible. So exorbitant an amount would be out of all proportion to the Jewish taxes in other cities of which we have evidence.

[225] M. Wiener, l. c., p. 175, No. 490.

[226] *Chroniken Deutscher Staedte*, V, p. 374.

[227] Reinertshofer, l. c., p. 16.

[228] I. Kracauer, *Geschichte der Juden in Frankfurt am Main*, I (1925), p. 170.

[229] M. Wiener, l. c., p. 194, No. 587. The abolition of juridical autonomy preceded the Jewish expulsion in Regensburg also; see Straus II.

[230] *Zeitschrift für die gesamten Staatswissenschaften*, XXVII, p. 302.

[231] *Chroniken deutscher Städte*, V, pp. 437, 22. Also K. Mohr, *Die Anfänge der modernen Warenspekulation* (1927), p. 16.

[232] R. Grünfeld, l. c., p. 34 ff.

[233] M. Wiener, p. 203, No. 636; *Chroniken Deutscher Städte*, IV, p. 326.

[234] Reinertshofer, l. c., p. 18; Wiener, l. c., passim.

[235] Straus I.

[236] *"Lebendiges Geleit"* was the term applied to safe conduct by a watchman or guardian.

[237] Bisle, *Die öffentliche Armenpflege* (1904), p. 19.

[238] P. von Stetten, l. c., p. 538.

[239] Ib. p. 611. This corresponded to the Jewish garb customary in Rome. It was introduced in Augsburg by a Dioccsan Synod of that city held in 1452.

[240] Bisle, l. c. As the above citation shows that the right of domicile was accorded to five Jews only, these statements are open to question.

[241] P. von Stetten, l. c., passim.

[242] F. I. Schöningh, *Die Rehlinger in Augsburg* (1927), pp. 55, 99.

[243] P. von Stetten, l. c., II, pp. 109, 1099.

[244] P. Dirr, in *Zeitschrift des Historischen Vereins für Schwaben und Neuburg*, l. c., pp. 37, 79.

[245] R. Hipper, *Die Reichstadt Augsburg und die Judenschaft von Beginn des 18. Jhdts. bis zur Aufhebung der reichstädtischen Verfassung* (Erlangen Dissertation, 1923), p. 145.

[246] In the sequel: Kr.=Kriegshaber, Pf.=Pfersee, St.=Steppach.

[247] Hipper, l. c., p. 94.

[248] Ib. p. 58.

[249] J. J. Moser, *Von den teutschen Reichstägen* (1774), I, p. 273.

[250] P. von Stetten, l. c., p. 30.

[251] In the year 1751 distinctions were made between 1. Imperial and princely Jews; 2. Jews dependent on the higher authorities and citizens; 3. Jews without privileges. These three classes had different political status.

[252] P. von Stetten, l. c., pp. 37, 55. Cf. Hipper, l. c., p. 54.

[253] Ib. II, p. 589.

[254] Hipper, l. c., p. 67.

[255] Ib. p. 20.

[256] Ib. p. 140.

[257] Cf. A. Dietz, *Frankfurter Handelsgeschichte*, IV, p. 456.

[258] Buff, in *Sammler* (1882), No. 108.

[259] P. von Stetten, l. c., p. 21; Hipper, l. c., p. 139 ff.

[260] *Chronicle of Ber Bernhard Ulmann, 1803* (a mistake for 1804). Privately printed by Carl J. Ulmann, New York, 1928.

[261] Hipper, l. c., p. 141.

[262] An Austrian general made the following statement at that time regarding the situation in Augsburg: "The old inimical attitude toward the Jews, which in any event is no longer consistent with the spirit of our age, might have some merit in times of peace but should not be taken so seriously in times of war." Hipper, l. c., p. 121.

[263] See above.

[264] In 1762, we are told, many Jews married their children to persons in Hamburg and Frankfort. Reinertshofer, l. c., p. 38.

[265] Hipper, l. c., p. 138.

[266] Reinertshofer, l. c., p. 44.

[267] L. Huemmert, *Die finanziellen Beziehungen jüdischer Bankiers und Heereslieferanten zum bayerischen Staat in der 1. Hälfte des 19. Jahrhunderts* (1927), p. 12; Wagenseil, l. c., IV, p. 140.

[268] P. von Stetten, l. c., p. 51.

[269] Wagenseil, l. c., p. 140.

[270] Reinertshofer, l. c., p. 43.

[271] The total numbers in what follows refer to Kriegshaber, Pfersee and Steppach together.

[272] A. Kohut, l. c., p. 659, not giving his sources.

[273] See above. In the year 1745 Jacob Baumgarten wrote (*Theologische Bedenken*, p. 37): "Most Jews can read German very poorly, but cannot write." The above mentioned proselyte, Ch. W. Christlieb, could not write German either.

[274] See above.

[275] P. von Stetten, l. c., p. 70.

[276] F. M. Hoscher, *Rückerinnerung an die Stadt Augsburg* (1807), p. 45.

[277] Concerning the intellectual development in the 19th century see above. The Berlin dissertation (1933) of S. Bromberger on the early history of the Jews in Regensburg (the early Middle Ages) was not known to the author until after this work was finished.

INDEX

249